Guided Meditations for Young Catholics

Glynnis Hope B. Dawson

Music composed by John Dawson

NOVALIS

Cover design: Martin Gould
Layout: Audrey Wells
Interior photos: p. 11: iStockphoto; pp. 25, 109: W.P. Wittman; pp. 41, 61, 91: Jupiter Images

Published by Novalis

Publishing Office
10 Lower Spadina Avenue, Suite 400
Toronto, Ontario, Canada
M5V 2Z2

Head Office
4475 Frontenac Street
Montréal, Québec, Canada
H2H 2S2

www.novalis.ca

Library and Archives Canada Cataloguing in Publication

Dawson, Glynnis Hope, 1979-
Guided meditations for young Catholics / Glynnis Hope B. Dawson ; music composed by John Dawson.

Accompanied by a compact disc. ISBN 978-2-89646-409-8

1. Meditations. I. Dawson, John, 1975- II. Title.

BX2182.3.D39 2013 242 C2013-901699-6

Printed in Canada.

We acknowledge the financial support of the Government of Canada through the Canada Book Fund for business development activities.

5 4 3 2 1 17 16 15 14 13

Table of Contents

Introduction

As Catholic educators and youth ministers, we are constantly striving to find ways of teaching our young people that God is present in all that we say and do. Looking at the world today, we see many challenges that force us to ask ourselves, "How can we make God relevant to the young Catholics in our lives? How can we introduce prayer to youth in a non-threatening way that allows them to take ownership of their faith and their prayer life?"

Guided Meditations for Young Catholics aims at helping the catechist, youth minister and classroom teacher to guide young people to develop skills for settling the body and mind to prepare for prayer. Breathing slowly, concentrating on the intake and release of breath, focusing on a prayerful word, listening to prayerful music, and carefully listening to the words of the "guide" are tools that young Catholics can use to enrich and deepen their prayer life.

In providing teachers, catechists and youth ministers with opportunities to lead young people in prayer, we hope that this resource acts as a stepping stone, so that in time, each individual takes ownership of their prayer life. This book is not intended to replace the beautiful prayers of our Catholic tradition; rather, it is designed to offer our young people an additional form of prayer. They will discover that there are many ways to pray, and that each type of prayer opens different avenues that will lead them closer to God. Through contemplation and discernment, as well as wonder and awe of the world around them, they will build and strengthen their relationship with God, who loves them unconditionally.

You may wonder, "How will I find the time to introduce another form of prayer? I am asked to do so much, and my budget is so small!" Don't worry. With *Guided Meditations for Young Catholics,* all you need is a CD player and a space to gather; the meditation itself takes just a few minutes at the beginning or end of a class or gathering. Our youth who are inundated with a constant stream of thoughts and distractions, who are constantly multi-tasking in several areas, seldom have the opportunity to slow down and just "be." Meditation can teach young Catholics that there is merit to learning how to focus and how to be prayerful, if only for a few moments a day. This practice allows them to let their mind relax, to explore God's presence in all that they see and do, and, most of all, to learn more about themselves and their relationship to God and the world. It teaches them skills to settle their minds and to be fully present. It teaches them to look around and realize that there are so many wonderful things in the world to love and be grateful for, and that they, as young Catholics, can have a deep and meaningful relationship with God.

Catholic education is a joy as well as a challenge. We hope that this book can help you, as Catholic educators and youth ministers, to work towards helping our young people realize that it only takes a few moments of reflection and prayer to find God in a very busy world.

Thank you for all that you do.

God bless,

Glynnis Hope B. Dawson
and John Dawson

How to Use *Guided Meditations for Young Catholics*

Guided Meditations for Young Catholics can be used at the beginning or at the end of a class or gathering – as a tool to focus the participants to review a topic that was covered on a previous day, or to consolidate what was discussed earlier. Whenever you choose to use it, we encourage you to offer them time to process their prayer through personal reflection. Further sharing with a partner and, later, within a larger group is ideal, as this will help them to process and synthesize what they have experienced in their prayer. But given the personal nature of meditation, this kind of sharing is always optional.

If your group has never done guided meditation before, you may want to practise the warm-up found at the beginning of all the meditations a few times first. That way they'll know what to expect and be able to relax and prepare for meditation.

Each meditation contains recommended pauses to allow participants time to reflect on what is said. As the catechist or youth minister, you know your group and its needs best. Please feel free to adapt these meditations to suit the group by adjusting the timing of how you read each meditation or adding (or taking away) some reflections, depending on what works for your group. Be sure to read through the meditation before you use it, as some topics raised (e.g., drugs, sexuality) may not be suitable for younger participants who have not dealt with these subjects in a faith context before.

The reflection questions at the end of each guided meditation provide some ideas for encouraging participants to process and understand their thoughts and prayers. The discussion questions are intended to lead your group of young people into a deeper understanding of their relationship with God, themselves, friends, family and community. Adjust these questions as needed – pick and choose, or create your own.

How to Pace the Guided Meditation

When leading a guided meditation, the pacing (how fast you read and how long you pause for participants to reflect between sentences) is very important. If you read too quickly, young people will not have enough time to follow through with what each meditation is asking them to reflect on. If you read too slowly, their minds will wander. We suggest that you wait at least five seconds (counting in your head: one, one thousand … two, one thousand … three, one thousand … four, one thousand … five, one thousand …) or more so all participants can follow the instructions as well as reflect. Watch your young people as you pause for moments of reflection. You can usually tell if they need more or less time by their facial expressions or body language.

Most of us learn best by doing. To prepare to guide your young people, have someone read the meditation to you so you can feel how much time you need to reflect. We also urge you to practise a few times with someone outside of your class or youth ministry setting; ask for feedback about whether your pacing helped to encourage their prayer and reflection.

Here is an example of how you could pace your guided meditation:

Find a comfortable position and settle in … *(allow participants some time to get comfortable)* …

take a nice, deep breath and let the air flow slowly out of your lungs … (5 seconds) … do this again, paying special attention to the air as you inhale … (5 seconds) … and as you exhale … (5 seconds) … inhale … (5 seconds) … exhale … (5 seconds) … inhale … (5 seconds) … exhale … (5 seconds) …

now, as you take a deep breath, I want you to hold it and scrunch up your toes as tightly as you can … (5 seconds) … now breathe out and relax your toes … (5 seconds) …

this time, take a deep breath and flex your calves … (5 seconds) … hold it … (5 seconds) … and relax … (5 seconds) …

deep breath and tighten your thighs … hold it … (5 seconds) … relax … (5 seconds) …

deep breath and tighten your stomach … (5 seconds) … hold it … (5 seconds) … and relax … (5 seconds) …

take a deep breath and make the tightest fists possible … (5 seconds) … hold it … (5 seconds) … and relax … (5 seconds) …

deep breath and stretch your arms so they're tight … (5 seconds) … hold it … (5 seconds) … and relax … (5 seconds) …

now take a deep breath and bring your shoulders right up to your ears … (5 seconds) … hold it … (5 seconds) … and relax … (5 seconds) …

take a deep breath and scrunch up your face … (5 seconds) … hold it … (5 seconds) … and relax … (5 seconds) …

take a deep breath and tense up your whole body … (5 seconds) … from the tips of your toes, through your legs, your stomach, your arms and your face … (5 seconds) … hold it … (5 seconds) … and relax … (5 seconds) …

now, as you relax, concentrate on your breathing … (5 seconds) … inhale … (5 seconds) … exhale … (5 seconds) … inhale … (5 seconds) … exhale … (5 seconds) … as you inhale, think "Holy" … (5 seconds) … and as you exhale, think "Spirit" … *(allow participants enough time to think of the Holy Spirit for a few breaths)* …

Once you have found the right rhythm for leading the meditation, and have practised it yourself (both as participant and as leader), you are ready to start!

Thirty-nine meditations on a range of themes are provided – from key aspects and experiences of young people's lives, to the liturgical seasons of Advent/Christmas and Lent/Easter, to the gifts and the fruits of the Holy Spirit, to faith in action.

Incorporating the Music CD

This resource comes with a CD containing nine original compositions of meditative music. Here are some suggestions for which track to use with which meditations:

Track 1: **Warm-up – Longer**
(A bell chimes three times followed by a repetitive, calming series of chords set to a relaxed breathing pace)

Track 2: **Warm-up – Shorter**
(Same as Track 1, but about half as long, for teachers who wish to do a shorter warm-up)

Note: Track 1 or 2 is meant to be played as part of the general centering activity before the meditation itself begins.

Track 3: **Meditation I**
Theme: Myself

Track 4: **Meditation II**
Theme: Gifts of the Holy Spirit

Track 5: **Meditation III**
Theme: Lent

Track 6: **Meditation IV**
Theme: Lent, particularly Good Friday

Track 7: **Meditation V**
Theme: Easter, and the Fruits of the Holy Spirit

Track 8: **Meditation VI**
Theme: Advent

Track 9: **Meditation VII**
Theme: Late Advent/Christmas, Easter, and Faith in Action

An icon indicating which track to use is found at the start of each meditation.

Myself

WARM-UP

Track 1 or Track 2

Find a comfortable position and settle in ... (*allow participants some time to get comfortable*) ... take a nice, deep breath and let the air flow slowly out of your lungs ... do this again, paying special attention to the air as you inhale ... and as you exhale ... inhale ... exhale ... inhale ... exhale ... now, as you take a deep breath, I want you to hold it and scrunch up your toes as tightly as you can ... breathe out and relax ... this time, take a deep breath and flex your calves ... hold it ... and relax ... deep breath and tighten your thighs ... hold it ... and relax ... deep breath and tighten your stomach ... hold it ... and relax ... take a deep breath and make the tightest fists possible ... hold it ... and relax ... deep breath and stretch your arms until they're tight ... hold it ... and relax ... now take a deep breath and bring your shoulders right up to your ears ... hold it ... and relax ... take a deep breath and scrunch up your face ... hold it ... and relax ... and take a deep breath and tense up your whole body ... from the tips of your toes, through your legs, your stomach, your arms and your face ... hold it ... and relax ... now, as you relax, concentrate on your breathing ... inhale ... exhale ... inhale ... exhale ...

A New School Year: As you inhale, think "Jesus" ... and as you exhale, think "Jesus" ... (*allow participants enough time to think of Jesus for a few breaths*) ...

Family: As you inhale, think "love" ... and as you exhale, think "love" ... (*allow participants enough time to think of love for a few breaths*) ...

Friends: As you inhale, think "love" ... and as you exhale, think "love" ... (*allow participants enough time to think of love for a few breaths*) ...

Gifts and Talents: As you inhale, think "Holy" ... and as you exhale, think "Spirit" ... (*allow participants enough time to think of the Holy Spirit for a few breaths*) ...

End of the School Year: As you inhale, think "Jesus" ... and as you exhale, think "Jesus" ... (*allow participants enough time to think of Jesus for a few breaths*) ...

A New School Year

Track 3

Begin with the warm-up for this section, then move into the meditation:

Take a moment to think about your summer ... what were some of your favourite memories? ... what made these memories so special? ... have you changed in any ways over the summer? ... what will you miss most about being on holidays compared to being at school? ...

For some, a new school year can be very exciting, while for others it can be terrifying and anxiety ridden ... have you been enjoying the first (few) day(s) of school? ... what makes this time great or not so great? ... there are always a lot of questions as a new school year begins. Let's take a few minutes to reflect silently ...

Are you excited about your new teacher(s)? ... are you happy with the other students who are in your class? ... are you excited about being in a new grade (or class)? why or why not? ... what are some things that you are dreading, or are nervous about? ... can you anticipate any new expectations people will have of you this year?

The beginning of a school year is an opportunity for change ... what are some things that you'd like to do differently this year compared to last year? ... what kinds of actions can you take to make these desires for change a reality? ... who can you turn to for help if you have a hard time with these changes?...

(Pause for about 10 to 20 seconds before giving the next set of instructions)

Bring your consciousness back to your focus word … *Jesus* … Now, as you breathe in, concentrate on the name *Jesus* … and as you breathe out, concentrate on *Jesus* … (*allow participants to take a few breaths*). Begin to wiggle your toes, your fingers. When you are ready, open your eyes and slowly sit up. Please remain quiet until we are ready to reflect on our meditation.

Reflection / Discussion Questions:

1. What were some of the highlights of your summer?
2. Are you anxious or excited about this new school year? Explain your thinking.
3. Think of three strategies you can use to help you succeed at school this year. Write each one on a sticky note and stick it in your agenda or in your locker so you see them often.

Family

Track 3

Begin with the warm-up for this section, then move into the meditation:

Imagine that it is a beautiful, sunny day … it's not too hot, and it's not too cold … it's the perfect weather after a long winter, where it's warm enough that you don't need to wear a thick jacket, but it's cool enough that you're not going to overheat … you pause for a moment and close your eyes … with your eyes shut, you can feel the warmth of the sun on you … and the sounds around your neighbourhood are easier to pick out … perhaps you hear a bird … or the cars driving by … perhaps you hear some people walking and chatting near you … when you open your eyes, you notice that you are not alone … there, joining you on your walk, is Jesus … he says, "Hello," … and you say, "Hi" … you two walk in silence for awhile, just enjoying being outside … there really is no pressure from him to say anything, which is kind of nice … but for some reason, you start chatting away with him … perhaps it's because walking with Jesus makes you feel so comfortable, you can't help but share the things on your mind … you tell him about the things you're grateful for … and the things you're struggling with … next, you start talking about the people in your family … what you love about each of them … and what drives you crazy … the whole time Jesus walks by your side, you notice how focused he is on what you're saying … he doesn't interrupt, or jump in to tell you what to do … he just listens … you explain how sometimes you do things to your family that you're not proud of … sometimes you have a hard time apologizing to them … but at other times, you are incredible and have a great time with your family … you talk about how your family has changed since you were little … what you miss and don't miss about that time … even though your family isn't perfect, you know that when you get older, you'll have some positive memories to look back on … you stop talking almost as quickly as you started … you continue to reflect silently about your relationship with the members of your family … you think about how your family is unique and unlike any other that you know … when your thoughts about your family stop, you look over at Jesus and he finally speaks … and because he is talking so quietly, you have to lean in a bit so you can hear what he has to say about you and your family … when he's finished speaking to you, the two of you continue your walk in silence … once you've gathered your thoughts, you look up and realize that you've somehow ended up back home … waving goodbye to Jesus, you thank him for listening … he thanks you for walking and talking … and you both go on your way …

(Pause for about 10 to 20 seconds before giving the next set of instructions)

Bring your consciousness back to your focus word … *love* … Now, as you breathe in, concentrate on the word *love* … and as you breathe out, concentrate on *love* … (*allow participants to take a few breaths*). Begin to wiggle your toes, your fingers. When you are ready, open your eyes and slowly sit up. Please remain quiet until we are ready to reflect on our meditation.

Reflection / Discussion Questions:

1. How would you describe your relationships with your family members? Try to think of one or two words for each one.
2. What do you like about how you are with the members of your family? Why?
3. What behaviours of yours would you like to change? How can you make this happen?

Friends

Track 3

Begin with the warm-up for this section, then move into the meditation:

It's another beautiful day … the sun is shining, the temperature outside is just as you like it, and you have time to be outside to enjoy the day! … you decide to go for a short walk … as you walk, you pay attention to all the little things in your neighbourhood that you usually pass by without a thought … you look at the buildings … and the trees … you notice the cars parked outside … and even notice some animals going about their business, doing what they do every day … you feel tired, so you find a nice place to sit or lie down to rest … you get comfortable and let your thoughts flow through your mind … you begin to think about you and your friends … there are so many things you love about your friends … you let your mind wander, thinking about the fun times you've had … and even the not so fun times … you think of what you like about your friends … and the things you wish they wouldn't do … you reflect on ways that you are similar to them … and you take time to think about how your friends have influenced you … have they helped you to be a better person? … or perhaps you've all made choices that may not have been wise … are there traits about them that you'd like to have as well? … what are they and why? … why do you think they're friends with you? … what do you have to offer to your friendship? … are they easy to get along with, or are you constantly arguing? … why? … do they help you to make good choices in your life? … do you all help each other to be better people? … take a moment to say a quiet prayer, asking Jesus to bless you and your friends … after checking the time, you realize it's time to go, so you slowly get up and go on your way …

(Pause for about 10 to 20 seconds before giving the next set of instructions)

Bring your consciousness back to your focus word … *love* … Now, as you breathe in, concentrate on the word *love* … and as you breathe out, concentrate on *love* … (*allow participants to take a few breaths*). Begin to wiggle your toes, your fingers. When you are ready, open your eyes and slowly sit up. Please remain quiet until we are ready to reflect on our meditation.

Reflection / Discussion Questions:

1. What are some of the qualities that you love about your friends?
2. In what ways do you and your friends help each other to do good things?
3. What qualities do you possess that make you a good friend?

Gifts and Talents

Track 3

Begin with the warm-up for this section, then move into the meditation:

When you were younger, it was pretty easy to know what you were good at ... maybe you were good at drawing or catching a ball, good at singing or making friends ... as you get older, it can be difficult to identify the many things that you're good at ... sometimes it's because people tell us that we're just not good enough and our feelings get hurt, but often it's because to develop a gift or talent is hard work ... God wants us to be happy and to feel like we can do things that make the people around us happy, too ... let's take a moment to reflect on our own gifts and talents ...

Think of some things that you're good at ... they can be things that everyone knows you can do ... but they can also be secret things that only you or some of the people closest to you know about ... how do you feel when you do these things? ... why do you think you feel this way? ... how would you feel if you couldn't do them anymore? ... why? ... has anyone helped you to develop your gift or talent? ... take a moment to think of them, or think of a person you'd like to have help you nurture your talent ... why do you think God wants us to share the gifts he's given us with the people around us? ... think of some ways that you can share your gifts with others and make a plan of action ...

Sometimes we are afraid to share our talents with others...why would someone be afraid to share their talents with people? ... is there a danger to keeping talents private? ... what are the advantages of keeping a talent to ourselves? ... Why do you think God wants us to share our gifts and talents with the people around us? …

(Pause for about 10 to 20 seconds before giving the next set of instructions)

Bring your consciousness back to your focus words … *Holy* … *Spirit* … Now, as you breathe in, concentrate on the word *Holy* … and as you breathe out, concentrate on *Spirit* … (*allow participants to take a few breaths*). Begin to wiggle your toes, your fingers. When you are ready, open your eyes and slowly sit up. Please remain quiet until we are ready to reflect on our meditation.

Reflection / Discussion Questions:

1. **1.** What were some of the gifts and talents you thought about during the guided meditation?
2. **2.** Who are the people who have helped you to develop these gifts and talents?
3. **3.** How can you use your gifts and talents to teach the world about God?

End of the School Year

Track 3

Begin with the warm-up for this section, then move into the meditation:

Imagine that you are standing just outside a park near your home … you decide to follow a path that takes you deeper into the park … you can hear your feet shuffling against the walkway … you smell the crisp air … you hear the faint sounds of the cars driving by in the distance; but more importantly, you hear the rustling of leaves in the trees and the birds calling to one another … as you walk further into the park, you look down and notice a dirt path that leads to a group of trees … you decide to allow your curiosity to lead you, and you follow the pathway into a small forest. Here, you notice the change in temperature … goosebumps quickly form on your arms … you decide to move briskly to keep warm, always following the path … as you walk, you gently push aside the wild growth of the trees and bushes, and take in the smell of the forest … it's a mixture of fresh dirt and crisp leaves along with a feeling of cool, refreshing moisture … you look behind you and realize that you have gone very deep into the forest … but you're not worried, because up ahead, you see that there's a garden where the sun is shining and many beautiful flowers are growing … you hear a trickling stream flowing in the distance … as you walk towards the garden, you feel the sun's warmth on your skin … happily, you enter the bright and beautiful garden and you hear your name being called gently … you turn around, and there, standing right in front you, is Jesus. He smiles at you and gestures for you to sit down with him … at once, as you sit down, you feel a sense of peace … he begins by telling you that he loves you and how happy he is that you have come to visit him … you feel at ease with Jesus' presence … you know that you can talk to him about anything and he'll listen and not judge you … you have a conversation with him and tell him everything that's on your mind … all that is happening in your life now … all the things that happened over the school year … when you have poured out all that you have to say to him, he smiles at you, and says that he is glad you came to visit him in his garden … he says that anytime you want, you can come to visit him to talk, or even to just sit together … you do not feel sad when it is time for you to go home, because you know that Jesus will always be here … after saying goodbye, you follow the path away from the garden and begin your journey home.

(Pause for about 10 to 20 seconds before giving the next set of instructions)

Bring your consciousness back to your focus word … *Jesus* … Now, as you breathe in, concentrate on the name *Jesus* … and as you breathe out, concentrate on *Jesus* … (*allow participants to take a few breaths*). Begin to wiggle your toes, your fingers. When you are ready, open your eyes and slowly sit up. Please remain quiet until we are ready to reflect on our meditation.

Reflection / Discussion Questions:

1. What were some of the things that you and Jesus talked about?
2. Did he say anything that surprised you? What was it?
3. What have you liked and disliked about guided meditation? Has it helped you to pray, and will you continue to reflect and have conversations with God?

Advent and Christmas

WARM-UP

Track 1 or Track 2

Find a comfortable position and setle in … (*allow participants some time to get comfortable*) … take a nice, deep breath and let the air flow slowly out of your lungs … do this again, paying special attention to the air as you inhale … and as you exhale … inhale … exhale … inhale … exhale … now, as you take a deep breath, I want you to hold it and scrunch up your toes as tightly as you can … breathe out and relax … this time, take a deep breath and flex your calves … hold it … and relax … deep breath and tighten your thighs … hold it … and relax … deep breath and tighten your stomach … hold it … and relax … take a deep breath and make the tightest fists possible … hold it … and relax … deep breath and stretch your arms until they're tight … hold it … and relax … now take a deep breath and bring your shoulders right up to your ears … hold it … and relax … take a deep breath and scrunch up your face … hold it … and relax … and take a deep breath and tense up your whole body … from the tips of your toes, through your legs, your stomach, your arms and your face … hold it … and relax … now, as you relax, concentrate on your breathing … inhale … exhale … inhale … exhale …

The Annunciation: As you inhale, think "love" … and as you exhale, think "love" … *(allow participants enough time to think of love for a few breaths)* …

Advent 1: Hope – As you inhale, think "hope" … and as you exhale, think "hope" … *(allow participants enough time to think of hope for a few breaths)* …

Advent 2: Faith – As you inhale, think "faith" … and as you exhale, think "faith" … *(allow participants enough time to think of faith for a few breaths)* …

Advent 3: Joy – As you inhale, think "joy" … and as you exhale, think "joy" … *(allow participants enough time to think of joy for a few breaths)* …

Advent 4: Love – As you inhale, think "love" … and as you exhale, think "love" … *(allow participants enough time to think of love for a few breaths)* …

Christmas: As you inhale, think "Jesus" … and as you exhale, think "Jesus" … *(allow participants enough time to think of Jesus for a few breaths)* …

The Annunciation

Track 8

Begin with the warm-up for this section, then move into the meditation:

You are visiting Nazareth. Word has spread that Mary and Joseph have just gotten married … you are excited, so you decide to visit the newlyweds. When you knock on the door, Joseph answers and invites you in … he says that Mary has stepped out for a few moments, but you are welcome to stay for awhile … you follow him to the back of his home, and see some beautiful chairs and tables that he has been working on … taking a seat, you watch Joseph as he skillfully crafts one of four matching chair legs … just as with your closest friends, conversation flows easily between you and Joseph … as he works, he tells you about some things that happened to him and Mary … an angel had appeared to Mary and said to her, "Do not be afraid" … the angel continued, "You will conceive in your womb and bear a son … you will call him Jesus …" … you look at Joseph, who has stopped working at his bench for a moment. He looks at you and says quietly, "Mary said yes." … you take a second to digest all that Joseph has told you and you wonder, "How would I feel if an angel came and told me that God has a plan for me?" …"If the angel said God's plan involved me being judged by all the people around me, my friends, my family, and even strangers, would I say yes to God, just as Mary did? … Why?" … Joseph continues his story … he tells you that at first, he wasn't sure if he should marry her. But he also had a visit from an angel, only it was in his dreams … he relates part of his dream to you. The angels said to him, "*Do not be afraid to take Mary as your wife … for the child conceived in her is from the Holy Spirit. She will bear a son, and you are to name him Jesus …"* … again, Joseph's hands pause and he looks at you and says, "I did as the angel in my dream told me …" … and he smiles … just then, you notice that the smile isn't just because he was remembering his dream … you look behind you and there, you see Mary … you can see that she is pregnant … you stand up to greet her and congratulate her … she smiles and gives her belly a loving rub … "She said yes," you think to yourself … wow … Mary motions for you to come into the house and stay for supper. You accept, and you help her to prepare the meal …

(Pause for about 10 to 20 seconds before giving the next set of instructions)

Bring your consciousness back to your focus word … *love* … Now, as you breathe in, concentrate on the word *love* … and as you breathe out, concentrate on the word *love* (*allow participants to take a few breaths*). Begin to wiggle your toes, your fingers. When you are ready, open your eyes and slowly sit up. Please remain quiet until we are ready to reflect on our meditation.

Reflection / Discussion Questions:

1. If you were Joseph or Mary and an angel appeared to you saying that God would like you to do something special, would you accept? Why or why not? (Remember: God always gives us a choice!)
2. Imagine that you are either Mary or Joseph after the angel appears. Write a monologue of your thoughts about the event.
3. Would you do something for God even if it meant that people would look at you and judge you? Justify your response.

Advent 1: Hope

Track 8

This is the first week of Advent … this past Sunday at church, we lit the first candle on the Advent wreath … for some, this candle represents hope … we have many reasons to be hopeful at the beginning of the Advent season, but most of all, we hope for the coming of the Lord! … let us take a few moments to reflect on hope and the excitement of Jesus' approaching birth …

Imagine that you are sitting in your favourite spot in the world … you sit quietly and think about the word *hope* … what were some things that you remember being hopeful for when you were little? … what are some things that you are hopeful for now? … how are some of your hopes similar to when you were younger? … how are they different now? … have you ever had moments when you were lacking in hope?… what did you do when you felt hopeless? … what are some things you could do if you felt like you lacked hope? … many Christians consider themselves to be "people of hope" … take a moment to think of reasons why people would think of Christians as hopeful people … God promised his people that he would send Jesus, the Saviour of the world, and so the people waited in hope and anticipation for Jesus to come … take a moment to say a silent prayer to God as we wait in hope and anticipation for Christmas Day … Dear God, as the Christmas season begins, please help me to … I hope that … Thank you, God. Amen.

(Pause for about 10 to 20 seconds before giving the next set of instructions)

Bring your consciousness back to your focus word … *hope* … Now, as you breathe in, concentrate on the word *hope*

… and as you breathe out, concentrate on the word *hope* (*allow participants to take a few breaths*). Begin to wiggle your toes, your fingers. When you are ready, open your eyes and slowly sit up. Please remain quiet until we are ready to reflect on our meditation.

Reflection / Discussion Questions:

1. In your opinion, what is a good symbol of hope? Justify your answer using words, illustrations or both.
2. Why do you think the birth of Jesus is a symbol of hope?
3. Is it easy to be a hopeful person? Why or why not?

Advent 2: Faith

Track 8

Begin with the warm-up for this section, then move into the meditation:

This is the second week of Advent … on Sunday, we lit the second candle on the Advent wreath … this week, we will be thinking about faith … when we say that we have faith, it means we believe in something without looking for physical evidence … as we do the following meditation, ask yourself why John the Baptist is an excellent example of a person who has great faith …

Imagine that it is a beautiful, sunny day during Jesus' time … you have heard that John the Baptist has been baptizing people in the Jordan River near your home … many of your friends have gone to hear him talk, while others have asked John the Baptist to baptize them … you decide to go and hear him speak … you still aren't sure if you want to be baptized by him, but you are curious to see why so many people speak so highly of him … as you approach the place, you can see many of your friends and neighbours, but also people you don't recognize … you hear John speaking in a clear and gentle voice … "*Prepare the way of the Lord, make his paths straight … Every valley shall be filled, and every mountain and hill shall be made low … and the crooked shall be made straight, and the rough ways made smooth … and all flesh shall see the salvation of God*" … you have heard similar words from the Book of Isaiah … but somehow this time it sounds and means something different, coming from John the Baptist … he continues, "*Bear fruits worthy of repentance …*" … fruits of repentance? What does he mean? you ask yourself … maybe he wants you to feel sorry for the things you've done that aren't nice and to try to live a better life … John the Baptist continues, saying, "*Whoever has two coats must share with anyone who has none; and whoever has food must do likewise …*" … wow! What an extraordinary thing to say! You do a mental inventory of your belongings … what do you have that you can share with those in need? … you hear a buzz among the crowd: "Do you think John could be the Messiah? The one we've been waiting for?" … could he be the one, you ask yourself? … but John, overhearing what people were saying, called out in a clear voice, "*I baptize you with water; but one who is more powerful than I is coming …*" … "*I am not worthy to untie the thong of his sandals …*" … John knows that there will be someone more powerful than him? … who could that person be? … John continues to preach, but your mind is caught up with all that he has said so far. As the crowd begins to disperse, you walk away in silence, reflecting on all you have heard.

(Pause for about 10 to 20 seconds before giving the next set of instructions)

Bring your consciousness back to your focus word … *faith* … Now, as you breathe in, concentrate on the word *faith* … and as you breathe out, concentrate on the word *faith* (*allow participants to take a few breaths*). Begin to wiggle your toes, your fingers. When you are ready, open your eyes and slowly sit up. Please remain quiet until we are ready to reflect on our meditation.

Reflection / Discussion Questions:

1. In your opinion, what is a good symbol of faith? Justify your answer.
2. Do you have faith that God loves you? Explain your thinking.
3. God has faith in us. Do you agree or disagree? Why?

Advent 3: Joy

Track 8

Begin with the warm-up for this section, then move into the meditation:

On Sunday we lit the third candle, the pink one, on the Advent wreath … it was Gaudete [Gow-day-tay] Sunday … *Gaudete* is Latin for "joy" … this week we reflect on joy … imagine that you live in a community that has been visited by the Apostle Paul … during his visit, he spread the Good News about Christ … it has been several months since you have heard from him … suddenly, the news spreads among you and your friends that a letter from Paul has arrived … you and the other Christians in your community are invited to someone's house to hear what the letter says over a meal … as you gather with your friends around a dining room table, the excitement builds as someone takes out the letter, holds it up for everyone to see, and begins reading … what really makes you think are the last few lines of Paul's letter … "*Rejoice always … pray without ceasing … give thanks in all circumstances … for this is the will of God in Christ Jesus for you …*" … you ask yourself, how can I rejoice during the times that I am sad or frustrated? … is it possible to pray without ceasing? … how do I do that? … it's easy to give thanks when things are going my way, but how do I give thanks when things and people around me just don't seem to make me happy? … the letter goes on, saying, "*May the God of peace himself sanctify you entirely …*" … may God make me holy? Can I be special enough that God would want to do that to *me*? … why would God want to do that? … "*and may your spirit and soul and body be kept sound and blameless at the coming of our Lord Jesus Christ. The one who calls you is faithful, and he will do this ...*" ... you take a few moments to reflect on the letter in its entirety, and take a moment to say a silent prayer ... *rejoice always ... pray without ceasing ... give thanks in all circumstances* ... as you slowly open your eyes, you smile and see that you are not the only one who took time to pray quietly ... now that you have all heard the letter and had a few moments to reflect on it, you happily begin to chatter and continue sharing your meal ...

(Pause for about 10 to 20 seconds before giving the next set of instructions)

Bring your consciousness back to your focus word ... *joy* ... Now, as you breathe in, concentrate on the word *joy* ... and as you breathe out, concentrate on the word *joy* (*allow participants to take a few breaths*). Begin to wiggle your toes, your fingers. When you are ready, open your eyes and slowly sit up. Please remain quiet until we are ready to reflect on our meditation.

Reflection / Discussion Questions:

1. In your opinion, what is a good symbol of joy? Justify your answer.
2. St. Paul tells us in his letter to "rejoice always." Do you think it's possible to feel joy in all areas of your life at all times? Why or why not?
3. Write about a joyful moment in your life. What filled you with joy? Why?

Advent 4: Love

Track 9

Begin with the warm-up for this section, then move into the meditation:

It is now the last week of Advent … a week filled with love as we wait in anticipation for the coming of Christ … imagine what it must have been like to be Mary, waiting for Jesus to be born … you see Mary, sitting in her home, rubbing her large, pregnant belly … as you approach her, you overhear her gently speaking to her baby … not wanting to interrupt, you quietly stand aside, waiting for her to notice you … she looks up at you and, with a welcoming smile, she gestures for you to join her … you find a chair and sit close to her … you can feel her excitement … she tells you that she thinks she's going to have her baby soon … you listen as she tells you all the things she hopes for her child as he grows up … she is excited to finally meet him, and to hold him close … Mary can't wait to teach him and share things with him … she knows that her son is going to do many great things … and that he will teach her and those around them much, much more than she can ever imagine … she knows that he will lead many people to God … Mary can't wait to watch the things he will do as a baby … as a little boy … as a man … and she hopes that we will listen to her son because she knows in her heart that the blind will see … the lame will walk … the lepers will be healed … the deaf will hear … the dead will be raised … and the poor will have good news brought to them … when she pauses, she looks up … you follow her gaze and see Joseph, who was preparing for their trip to Bethlehem while you two were talking, standing nearby … he gently smiles at you and Mary … Joseph motions that it is time for them to start their journey … you stand up and thank Mary and Joseph for welcoming you into their home and go on your way …

(Pause for about 10 to 20 seconds before giving the next set of instructions)

Bring your consciousness back to your focus word … *love* … Now, as you breathe in, concentrate on the word *love* … and as you breathe out, concentrate on the word *love* (*allow participants to take a few breaths*). Begin to wiggle your toes, your fingers. When you are ready, open your eyes and slowly sit up. Please remain quiet until we are ready to reflect on our meditation.

Reflection / Discussion Questions:

1. In your opinion, what is a good symbol of love? Justify your answer.
2. How did you feel talking to Mary? Did she say anything that surprised you?
3. There are different kinds of love. There's the love we have for things like pizza or basketball. There's the romantic kind of love that we have for others. Finally, and most important, is the kind of love we have for people where we love and care for them because they are people and therefore made in the image of God. Explain why Advent is a good time to teach people about this last kind of love.

Christmas

Track 9

Begin with the warm-up for this section, then move into the meditation:

The Christmas season can be a busy and stressful time of the year … for some of us, the parties, decorating, cooking and shopping for gifts can be a ton of fun, while for others it can be overwhelming or maddening … as advertisers try to sell their products, we are made to believe that the central focus of Christmas is the presents we hope to get, and the presents we want to give … let us take a moment to meditate on the real reason for the season: the birth of Jesus! …

It is a cloudless night in Bethlehem … you, like many others, have returned from other towns for the census … you wonder if it could be true what the other guests in the inn have been saying: that a young woman gave birth to a baby boy in the stable … curiosity makes you climb out of your comfy bed, get dressed, and go for a walk around the inn to find the stable … as you approach it, you can feel that you are moving towards something special … you can't quite put your finger on what it is … perhaps it's the bright star shining above the stable … or maybe it's the way the animals are all gathered near the baby … or it's the tiny child, wrapped in a blanket in his mother's arms, as her husband stands nearby … whatever it is, you feel privileged to be witnessing this calm and beautiful scene … the young man looks up from where he is standing, and he proudly motions for you to enter and join them … quietly, you walk towards the sleeping child and his mother … you realize that you want to give the baby a present

… but what do you have to give? … you search your pockets and the things you have with you, and you find the perfect present … "His name is Jesus …" his mother says lovingly as she shows you the baby … you gently hand her your gift for the child as you repeat his name … "Jesus" … you smile as the young mother thanks you for the present … and at that moment, the baby opens his eyes and looks right at you, sweetly … "Hello, Jesus …" you say softly … you smile again, and with a courteous bow of your head to the new family, you return to your room in the inn …

(Pause for about 10 to 20 seconds before giving the next set of instructions)

Bring your consciousness back to your focus word … *Jesus* … Now, as you breathe in, concentrate on the name *Jesus* … and as you breathe out, concentrate on *Jesus* … (*allow participants to take a few breaths*). Begin to wiggle your toes, your fingers. When you are ready, open your eyes and slowly sit up. Please remain quiet until we are ready to reflect on our meditation.

Reflection / Discussion Questions:

1. What did you see, hear, smell and taste as you approached the stable? Did anything surprise you when you met Mary, Joseph and Jesus?
2. What was the perfect gift you found for Jesus?
3. What do you love about Christmas? What don't you like about Christmas? Write a monologue to share your thoughts.

Culminating Activities

1. Make a list of the symbols of Advent that each person has chosen. Invite them to draw or bring in their symbols to share with a partner, small group or the whole class. Ask them to explain why they chose these symbols.
2. Place the names of each person in the group on a sheet of paper and place them in a hat. Have every person pull out one name. Instead of exchanging presents, they are encouraged to do something kind or thoughtful for the person without letting them know they chose that person's name. You can extend this activity to last a week or longer, focusing on ways to learn about each other and build your community.
3. In the meditations, you focused on the words of Advent: hope, faith, joy and love. Ask participants to say which one is their favourite, and why.
4. As a group, celebrate an Advent mass or Liturgy of the Word. Find a way for everyone to participate.

The Gifts of the Holy Spirit

WARM-UP

Track 1 or Track 2

Find a comfortable position and settle in … *(allow participants some time to get comfortable)* … take a nice, deep breath and let the air flow slowly out of your lungs … do this again, paying special attention to the air as you inhale … and as you exhale … inhale … exhale … inhale … exhale … now, as you take a deep breath, I want you to hold it and scrunch up your toes as tightly as you can … breathe out and relax … this time, take a deep breath and flex your calves … hold it … and relax … deep breath and tighten your thighs … hold it … and relax … deep breath and tighten your stomach … hold it … and relax … take a deep breath and make the tightest fists possible … hold it … and relax … deep breath and stretch your arms until they're tight … hold it … and relax … now take a deep breath and bring your shoulders right up to your ears … hold it … and relax … take a deep breath and scrunch up your face … hold it … and relax … take a deep breath and tense up your whole body … from the tips of your toes, through your legs, your stomach, your arms and your face … hold it … and relax … now, as you relax, concentrate on your breathing … inhale … exhale … inhale … exhale … as you inhale, think "Holy" … and as you exhale, think "Spirit" … *(allow participants enough time to think of the Holy Spirit for a few breaths)* …

Wisdom

Track 4

Begin with the warm-up for this section, then move into the meditation:

There is a vast difference between being smart and being wise … a person who is smart is very good at understanding and remembering how things work, whereas a person who is wise can take information they have learned and apply it to everyday life … in the same way, the gift of Wisdom takes what we know is right and wrong and helps us to make decisions based on our knowledge of God and his desire for us to do good things … the gift of Wisdom can move us to take action to love those around us, especially those in need … let us take a moment to reflect on the gift of Wisdom …

Recall a time when you have been called upon to help someone who was having difficulty in their life … it could be a person you know or people in your community … or perhaps there was a natural disaster and your school helped people across the country or the world … what were some of the things that you, your family, church or school did to help these people? … what happened that made you, your family, church or school community feel moved to do something? … how did helping others help you to develop your wisdom of God's presence in the world? … what were some of the gifts or talents that people used to take the idea of helping others and make it a reality? … remember: sometimes it is the smallest of things that we do that can make the biggest difference, so try to think of specific things … if you're having a hard time finding an example, imagine how you could use your gifts or talents to help others …

Let us pray: O Holy Spirit, as I reflect on the gift of Wisdom, please help me to ... I hope that with this gift I will ... Thank you, Holy Spirit. Amen.

(Pause for about 10 to 20 seconds before giving the next set of instructions)

Bring your consciousness back to your focus words ... *Holy* ... *Spirit* ... Now, as you breathe in, concentrate on the word *Holy* ... and as you breathe out, concentrate on *Spirit* ... (*allow participants to take a few breaths*). Begin to wiggle your toes, your fingers. When you are ready, open your eyes and slowly sit up. Please remain quiet until we are ready to reflect on our meditation.

Reflection / Discussion Questions:

1. What are the characteristics of a wise person? Draw a person and label these characteristics on your drawing (e.g., eyes to see what is good and not so good in the world, a brain to decide what is right and wrong ...).
2. Do you think you are wise? Why or why not? Support your answer.
3. Think of one person in your life whom you think is wise. Why do you think he or she is a good example of a wise person?

Understanding

Track 4

Begin with the warm-up for this section, then move into the meditation:

The gift of Understanding helps us to believe in things not because we are told to, but bcause we know deep within us that something is good and true … When our daily decisions are made with this in mind, we are led closer to God … let us take a moment to reflect on the gift of Understanding …

Think of a time when you were out in the schoolyard or with your friends and you witnessed some bullying … did you say something to make it stop? … if you could go back, would you do something different to help the person who was being bullied? … why would you want to help them? … why is it important to help someone in need? … now think of a time when you may have bullied another person … what did you do? … why did you do it? … how did you feel afterwards and why? … if you could go back in time, would you do something different to the person you bullied? … now take a moment to think of a time when you were bullied by another person … how did it make you feel? … why do you think you felt that way? … if you could go back in time, would you do anything different? …

Let us pray: O Holy Spirit, as I prepare to receive the gift of Understanding, please help me to … I hope that with this gift I will … Thank you, Holy Spirit. Amen.

(Pause for about 10 to 20 seconds before giving the next set of instructions)

Bring your consciousness back to your focus words … *Holy* … *Spirit* … Now, as you breathe in, concentrate on the word *Holy* … and as you breathe out, concentrate on *Spirit* … (*allow participants to take a few breaths*). Begin to wiggle your toes, your fingers. When you are ready, open your eyes and slowly sit up. Please remain quiet until we are ready to reflect on our meditation.

Reflection / Discussion Questions:

1. What are the characteristics of an understanding person? Draw a person and label these characteristics on your drawing (e.g., a mind to know what is good and what is true, ears to listen to the truth, a heart that takes time to understand the world around them …).
2. How does showing understanding towards others bring you closer to God?
3. An understanding person will let people do whatever they want. Do you agree or disagree? Why or why not?

Counsel (Right Judgment)

Track 4

Begin with the warm-up for this section, then move into the meditation:

The gift of Counsel or Right Judgment helps us to know what is right and what is wrong ... when we exercise this gift, we choose to follow the teachings of Jesus and do what is good ... it is not always easy to make the right choices, but when we allow ourselves to be guided by the Holy Spirit, we can use our right judgment and feel good about our decisions ... fortunately for us, we have many examples of people who exemplified the gift of Counsel: the saints! ... many of them chose to do God's will, even if it meant that people made fun of them or thought they were strange ... let us take a moment to reflect on the gift of Judgment ...

Imagine that you are out with some friends at a party and someone offers you and your friends some drugs ... what would you do? ... have you taken time beforehand to think about what the drugs would do to your mind and body? ... would your decision change if you were offered drugs in front of people rather than if it was just you and another person? ... what decision do you think Jesus would make if he was in the same situation? ... why? ...

Let us pray: O Holy Spirit, As I prepare to receive the gift of Counsel, please help me to ... I hope that with this gift I will ... Thank you, Holy Spirit. Amen.

(Pause for about 10 to 20 seconds before giving the next set of instructions)

Bring your consciousness back to your focus words … *Holy* … *Spirit* … Now, as you breathe in, concentrate on the word *Holy* … and as you breathe out, concentrate on *Spirit* … (*allow participants to take a few breaths*). Begin to wiggle your toes, your fingers. When you are ready, open your eyes and slowly sit up. Please remain quiet until we are ready to reflect on our meditation.

Reflection / Discussion Questions:

1. What are the characteristics of a person with right judgment? Draw a person and label these characteristics on your drawing (e.g., a mind to discern what is right and wrong, a heart to judge with compassion …).
2. Think of at least three steps people your age can take to use good judgment. Why did you choose these steps?
3. Would you rather follow everyone else's judgment or your own? Which do you find easier? What are some consequences for both situations?

Knowledge

Track 4

Begin with the warm-up for this section, then move into the meditation:

The gift of Knowledge is more than knowing facts about God … it assists us in being aware of how God works in our lives, and where God is when things go well and also when life is difficult … learning to be aware and to accept that God is present in all things and in all aspects of our lives can bring us closer to God … let us take a moment to meditate on the gift of Knowledge …

Think of a time in your life when something wonderful happened to you … can you identify where God was at that time in your life? … if not, try to think of some of the good things that came about because of that something wonderful, or the people who were around you when this event occurred … how did you know God was there? … now think of a time when you were having some difficulty in your life … can you identify where God was when you were struggling? … who was there to help you? … what happened that made your difficulty a little bit better? … God often works in ways that we don't understand. As we allow ourselves to be open to the works of the Holy Spirit and the gift of Knowledge, it gets easier to notice that God is present in all aspects of our lives, whether we are happy or sad, triumphant or disappointed, hopeful or in despair …

Let us pray: O Holy Spirit, as I prepare to receive the gift of Knowledge, please help me to … I hope that with this gift I will … Thank you, Holy Spirit. Amen.

(Pause for about 10 to 20 seconds before giving the next set of instructions)

Bring your consciousness back to your focus words … *Holy* … *Spirit* … Now, as you breathe in, concentrate on the word *Holy* … and as you breathe out, concentrate on *Spirit* … (*allow participants to take a few breaths*). Begin to wiggle your toes, your fingers. When you are ready, open your eyes and slowly sit up. Please remain quiet until we are ready to reflect on our meditation.

Reflection / Discussion Questions:

1. What are the characteristics of a person who has knowledge? Draw a person and label these characteristics on your drawing (e.g., ears to hear the Good News, eyes to see God in the world around us …).
2. What are some things that you know are true about God? How do you know these things?
3. It's hard to be knowledgeable of God's presence in difficult life situations. Do you agree or disagree? Why?

Courage (Fortitude)

Track 4

Begin with the warm-up for this section, then move into the meditation:

For some of us, the gift of Courage or Fortitude comes easily, while for others, we must work to develop it … the gift of Courage usually comes to us when we least expect it … When something seems unfair, we sometimes feel moved to take action, to do something about it … for many of us, it can be a challenge to recognize times when we have been brave, but we have all been courageous at some point in our lives … what's important to remember is that sometimes, small acts of courage can make the biggest difference in our lives and the lives of those around us … we also need to remember that sometimes, all it takes to be courageous is to offer another person a random act of kindness …

Take a moment to think of a time when you have needed courage to do what was right … maybe you had to apologize for hurting a friend or family member's feelings … or maybe you helped someone out in the schoolyard … or perhaps another memory stands out in your mind … what made you feel like you had to take action? … were you scared? … Why or why not? … how did you feel afterwards? …

Let us pray: O Holy Spirit, as I prepare to receive the gift of Courage/Fortitude, please help me to … I hope that with this gift I will … Thank you, Holy Spirit. Amen.

(Pause for about 10 to 20 seconds before giving the next set of instructions)

Bring your consciousness back to your focus words … *Holy* … *Spirit* … Now, as you breathe in, concentrate on the word *Holy* … and as you breathe out, concentrate on *Spirit* … (*allow participants to take a few breaths*). Begin to wiggle your toes, your fingers. When you are ready, open your eyes and slowly sit up. Please remain quiet until we are ready to reflect on our meditation.

Reflection / Discussion Questions:

1. What are the characteristics of a courageous person? Draw a person and label these characteristics on your drawing (e.g., legs to stand up for what is good and right, hands to reach out to those in need …).
2. When have you shown courage? What do you think makes people stand up to do what is right or to do something good, even when others don't agree with them?
3. Think of someone in your life who is a good example of courage. What do they do that is courageous? Why do you think they are so brave?

Piety (Reverence)

Track 4

Begin with the warm-up for this section, then move into the meditation:

The gift of Piety or Reverence helps us to develop a deep sense of love and respect for God and the Church … it is more than being a person of devout prayer; the gift of Piety also helps us to put all our trust in the Lord, and to present ourselves wholeheartedly to God … let us take a moment to meditate on the gift of Piety …

Think of a time in your life when you have prayed to God … as you prayed, did you think of the words you were saying? … for practice, think of a prayer you know or a prayer that is in your heart and say it in your head slowly … now say the prayer in your head again, this time thinking of the words and what they mean … Take your time and allow your mind to focus on parts of the prayer that you feel are important to you … do the words connect you to God? … if yes, how do they connect you? … if not, which part(s) of the prayer make(s) you feel disconnected from God, and why? … How does or how can this prayer help you to develop a sense of love and respect for God? … what do you need to feel closer to God? …

Let us pray: O Holy Spirit, as I prepare to receive the gift of Wisdom, please help me to … I hope that with this gift I will … Thank you, Holy Spirit. Amen.

(Pause for about 10 to 20 seconds before giving the next set of instructions)

Bring your consciousness back to your focus words … *Holy … Spirit …* Now, as you breathe in, concentrate on the word *Holy* … and as you breathe out, concentrate on *Spirit* … (*allow participants to take a few breaths*). Begin to wiggle your toes, your fingers. When you are ready, open your eyes and slowly sit up. Please remain quiet until we are ready to reflect on our meditation.

Reflection / Discussion Questions:

1. What are the characteristics of a pious person? Draw a person and label these characteristics on your drawing (e.g., a heart to put trust in God, hands to pray …).
2. Think of the prayer you said in your head during your meditation. Why do you think saying it slowly and thinking of the words you're saying helps you be closer to God?
3. Being a reverent person is challenging. Do you agree or disagree? Why?

Wonder and Awe (Fear of the Lord)

Track 4

Begin with the warm-up for this section, then move into the meditation:

The gift of Wonder and Awe or Fear of the Lord allows us to be conscious of our surroundings and to appreciate the beauty around us … it moves us to do things, to see the dignity of the human person, to recognize the beauty of nature, and to identify that these things are the wonderful work of God … and we are grateful! The gift of Fear of the Lord doesn't mean we are afraid of God: it means we want to do things that will please God, just as we want to stay close to and do wonderful things for the people who are the most important in our lives … this gift gives us an urge to draw closer to God … when things are busy, as they often are, it's easy to forget that God is constantly showing us beautiful things, and that God is at the root of all this goodness … let us take a moment to reflect on the gift of Wonder and Awe …

Imagine a beautiful sunset … it can be one you've seen walking home at night, or a picture of a sunset that you have seen in a magazine or on TV … what made you think it was beautiful? … if you had to describe the sunset to someone who wasn't there at the time, what words would you use? … where can you find God's work in that sunset? … when you reflect on the sunset, do you feel closer to God? Why or why not? … How does the sunset make you feel? …

Let us pray: O Holy Spirit, as I prepare to receive the gift of Wonder and Awe/Fear of the Lord, please help me to … I hope that with this gift I will … Thank you, Holy Spirit. Amen.

(Pause for about 10 to 20 seconds before giving the next set of instructions)

Bring your consciousness back to your focus words … *Holy* … *Spirit* … Now, as you breathe in, concentrate on the word *Holy* … and as you breathe out, concentrate on *Spirit* … (*allow participants to take a few breaths*). Begin to wiggle your toes, your fingers. When you are ready, open your eyes and slowly sit up. Please remain quiet until we are ready to reflect on our meditation.

Reflection / Discussion Questions:

1. What are the characteristics of a person who sees the world with wonder and awe? Draw a person and label these characteristics on your drawing (e.g., eyes to see the beauty in the world, ears to hear the amazing world around us, and a mouth to share with others the things we find wonderful in the world …).
2. How would you explain wonder and awe to friend? To a Grade 1 student? To an adult?
3. When we see beautiful things, we get a glimpse of God. Do you agree or disagree? Explain your answer.

Using the Gifts of the Holy Spirit

Track 4

Begin with the warm-up for this section, then move into the meditation:

Let us take some time to meditate on the Gifts of the Holy Spirit ... may the gift of Wisdom help you take what you have learned and apply it to everyday life ... may this gift help you to discern what is right and wrong ... may it help you to make decisions that are good and will bring you closer to God ... May the gift of Understanding help you to believe in God not because you are told to, but because you know deep in your heart and soul that God is good and wants good things for you ... May the gift of Counsel/Right Judgment give you the strength to know what is right and what is wrong ... may you try your best to choose to do the right thing, even if those around you choose otherwise ... May the gift of Knowledge help you to be aware of God in all things that you do, say, see and hear ... May the gift of Courage/Fortitude guide you to be strong to stand up for what is right ... May the gift of Piety/Reverence help you to develop a close, loving relationship with God ... May the gift of Wonder and Awe/Fear of the Lord help you to be aware of God's active participation to make the world beautiful for us to live in ... and may the Holy Spirit bless you and guide you as you prepare to receive the sacrament of Confirmation ...

Let us pray: O Holy Spirit, as I prepare for the sacrament of Confirmation, please help me to ... I hope that this sacrament will ... Thank you, Holy Spirit. Amen.

(Pause for about 10 to 20 seconds before giving the next set of instructions)

Bring your consciousness back to your focus words ... *Holy* ... *Spirit* ... Now, as you breathe in, concentrate on the word *Holy* ... and as you breathe out, concentrate on *Spirit* ... (*allow participants to take a few breaths*). Begin to wiggle your toes, your fingers. When you are ready, open your eyes and slowly sit up. Please remain quiet until we are ready to reflect on our meditation.

Reflection / Discussion Questions:

1. What are the characteristics of a person who uses all seven Gifts of the Holy Spirit? Draw a person and label these characteristics on your drawing (e.g., arms to reach out to those in need, ears to hear the Word of God, an eyebrow to raise when there are things we need to reflect on ...).
2. What gifts do you find come easily to you? Which ones are more challenging? What can you do to develop them?

Culminating Activities

1. Create a picture book, web page, or slideshow that illustrates the seven Gifts of the Holy Spirit for young children. How would you explain them in a way that a child would understand?
2. Create a comic book using the Gifts of the Holy Spirit as superhero characters. What would they look like? Who would be the villains?
3. Write a song to teach people about the Gifts of the Holy Spirit. Choose your audience: children, teens or adults. Create a video to share your song with others.
4. Design a game that can teach children about the Gifts of the Holy Spirit that is hands-on and allows the kids to be physically active. Consider using a ball, skipping rope or other equipment as well as music. Test it out with your peers.

The Fruits of the Holy Spirit

WARM-UP

Track 1 or Track 2

Find a comfortable position and settle in … *(allow participants some time to get comfortable)* … take a nice, deep breath and let the air flow slowly out of your lungs … do this again, paying special attention to the air as you inhale … and as you exhale … inhale … exhale … inhale … exhale … now, as you take a deep breath, I want you to hold it and scrunch up your toes as tightly as you can … breathe out and relax … this time, take a deep breath and flex your calves … hold it … and relax … deep breath and tighten your thighs … hold it … and relax … deep breath and tighten your stomach … hold it … and relax … take a deep breath and make the tightest fists possible … hold it … and relax … deep breath and stretch your arms until they're tight … hold it … and relax … now take a deep breath and bring your shoulders right up to your ears … hold it … and relax … take a deep breath and scrunch up your face … hold it … and relax … and take a deep breath and tense up your whole body … from the tips of your toes, through your legs, your stomach, your arms and your face … hold it … and relax … now, as you relax, concentrate on your breathing … inhale … exhale … inhale … exhale … as you inhale, think "Holy" … and as you exhale, think "Spirit" … *(allow participants enough time to think of the Holy Spirit for a few breaths)* …

Charity

Track 7

Begin with the warm-up for this section, then move into the meditation:

When you think of charity, what comes to mind? … there are many charities that work towards helping others … at Confirmation, we are encouraged to nurture the gifts that the Holy Spirit bestows on us, so we can be closer to God … these gifts move us to take action, to help those in need … but the fruit of Charity is more than raising money, volunteering our time and organizing special events … as young Catholics, you are also called to draw closer to God through prayer … let us take a moment to reflect on this fruit of the Holy Spirit: Charity …

Think of time when you tried to help someone … it can be a friend, a family member, or an organized charity that helps in your community or around the world … what did they need? … why did they need your help? … how did you try to help? … now think about what you did … make a connection between you and God. In other words, how did your actions demonstrate God's love for people in the world? … take a moment to think about how your actions brought you closer to God and gave you a better understanding of God's love for people (you may not have noticed that your actions brought you closer to God when you were doing them, so try to identify how doing something good helped you to get to know God unconsciously) …

Now take a moment and think of a time when someone tried to help you when you were in need … how did it make you feel? … has anyone ever tried to help you when you didn't need any help? … how did that make you feel? …

can you tell when someone genuinely wants to help you and when they're just doing it because they have to? …

Let us pray: O Holy Spirit, please help me to use your gifts to be charitable to those around me … help me to be conscious of you working through me, and help me to draw closer to God … I ask this through Christ our Lord. Amen.

(Pause for about 10 to 20 seconds before giving the next set of instructions)

Bring your consciousness back to your focus words … *Holy* … *Spirit* … Now, as you breathe in, concentrate on the word *Holy* … and as you breathe out, concentrate on *Spirit* … (*allow participants to take a few breaths*). Begin to wiggle your toes, your fingers. When you are ready, open your eyes and slowly sit up. Please remain quiet until we are ready to reflect on our meditation.

Reflection / Discussion Questions:

1. Why do you think we should show charity to those who need it?
2. Do you have a charity or organization that you are passionate about? What is it and what does it do?
3. Draw something that you think symbolizes charity. Explain why you chose this symbol.

Joy

Track 7

Begin with the warm-up for this section, then move into the meditation:

What comes to mind when you think of the word *joy*? … for Christians, joy is more than being happy … it is present in all aspects of our lives: when life is going great, when life is challenging, and when life is somewhere in between … let us take a moment to meditate on this fruit of the Holy Spirit …

Joy brings us hope and delight in the world … it becomes part of our attitude for life … with help from the Gifts that the Holy Spirit bestows on us, we can learn that to be joyful is to be aware of God in all aspects of our lives … let us take a moment to reflect on our own times of joy …

Think of a time when you have felt joyful … we can feel an overwhelming amount of joy in simple things, like taking a younger cousin to play at the park, or we can feel joy in big events, like when we excel in an activity that we have worked hard to become an expert in … now try to think about where God was when you felt this way …

Let us pray: O Holy Spirit, please help me to use your gifts to be joyful at all times in my life … help me to be conscious of you working through me, and help me to draw joyfully closer to God … I ask this through Christ our Lord. Amen.

(Pause for about 10 to 20 seconds before giving the next set of instructions)

Bring your consciousness back to your focus words … *Holy* … *Spirit* … Now, as you breathe in, concentrate on the word *Holy* … and as you breathe out, concentrate on *Spirit* … (*allow participants to take a few breaths*). Begin to wiggle your toes, your fingers. When you are ready, open your eyes and slowly sit up. Please remain quiet until we are ready to reflect on our meditation.

Reflection / Discussion Questions:

1. Name a time when you have felt joyful. Where were you, what were you doing, what made you so happy, and how did the people around you feel?
2. Can you be joyful even if you're sad? Explain your answer.
3. Draw something that you think symbolizes joy. Explain why you chose this symbol.

Peace

Track 7

Begin with the warm-up for this section, then move into the meditation:

What do you think of when you reflect on peace? ... for us Christians, peace is more than just quiet, or the absence of war ... we think of peace in all aspects of our lives: our homes, communities and relationships, but also in our hearts and minds ... when we have peace, it leaves us open to listening intently for God, and all that God has to say and do in our lives ... let us take a moment to reflect on this fruit of the Holy Spirit ...

What are some images that make you think of peace, or make you feel peaceful? ... where is God in the peaceful things you see? ... try your best to be as specific as you can ... are there things you enjoy doing that help you to feel peaceful? ... if so, take some time to reflect on them ... where is God in the things you love to do? ... think of a person you think is a good representative of peace ... where is God in the peaceful people you know in your life? ... now take a moment to reflect on your life ... do you have peace in your life? ... are your relationships with your friends, family, teachers and your priest peaceful? ... if they are, how do you create that peace? ... if not, what would you like to do to help your relationships become more peaceful? ... peace isn't always easy ... it takes the Holy Spirit to work through us to make it a reality ...

Let us pray: O Holy Spirit, please help me to use your gifts to bring peace to my life and to those around me ... help me to be conscious of you working through me, and help me to draw closer to God ... I ask this through Christ our Lord. Amen.

(Pause for about 10 to 20 seconds before giving the next set of instructions)

Bring your consciousness back to your focus words ... *Holy* ... *Spirit* ... Now, as you breathe in, concentrate on the word *Holy* ... and as you breathe out, concentrate on *Spirit* ... (*allow participants to take a few breaths*). Begin to wiggle your toes, your fingers. When you are ready, open your eyes and slowly sit up. Please remain quiet until we are ready to reflect on our meditation.

Reflection / Discussion Questions:

1. Write a poem about peace and illustrate it.
2. You can only have peace when everything is quiet and still. Do you agree or disagree with this statement? Why?
3. Draw something that you think symbolizes peace. Explain why you chose this symbol.

Patience

Track 7

Begin with the warm-up for this section, then move into the meditation:

Have you ever heard the saying "Patience is a virtue"? ... have you ever thought about what that really means? ... to be patient can be described as waiting without being annoyed or angry, no matter how long it takes ... it's not easy, is it? ... let us take a moment to reflect on this fruit of the Holy Spirit ...

Are you a patient person? why or why not? ... what are some things you are good at waiting for? ... what are some things you find challenging to be patient for? ... are there some things that make you feel impatient? ... are there some people who seem to bring out the impatient side of you? ... why do you get annoyed or angry? ... think of at least three proactive things you can do to help yourself learn to be able to wait for things to happen without getting annoyed ... why do you think we need the Gifts of the Holy Spirit to help us learn to be more patient? ... how can being patient help us to develop our relationship with God? ...

Let us pray: O Holy Spirit, please help me to use your gifts to be more patient with myself, with others and with the things in my life ... help me to be conscious of you working through me, and help me to draw closer to God ... I ask this through Christ our Lord. Amen.

(Pause for about 10 to 20 seconds before giving the next set of instructions)

Bring your consciousness back to your focus words ... *Holy* ... *Spirit* ... Now, as you breathe in, concentrate on the word *Holy* ... and as you breathe out, concentrate on *Spirit* … (*allow participants to take a few breaths*). Begin to wiggle your toes, your fingers. When you are ready, open your eyes and slowly sit up. Please remain quiet until we are ready to reflect on our meditation.

Reflection / Discussion Questions:

1. Write a "recipe" for patience. What steps should people take to develop the fruit of patience?
2. Are there times when you should be allowed to be impatient? Explain your thinking.
3. Draw something that you think symbolizes patience. Explain why you chose this symbol.

Kindness

Track 7

Begin with the warm-up for this section, then move into the meditation:

As Christians, we are all called to be kind … when we nurture the gifts that the Holy Spirit bestows on us during our Confirmation, we find ourselves trying to do kind acts for others in all that we say, in all that we think and in all that we do … we are moved to be kind, and in many ways, this kindness is really a love for ourselves and others … after all, in the Bible, Jesus tells us to treat others as we ourselves would like to be treated … who among us would object to being treated with kindness? … let us take a moment to reflect on this fruit of the Holy Spirit …

Do you strive to be kind in all that you say? … think of some of the kind things you have said to and about others … do you try to be kind in all that you think? … think of some kind things that you have thought lately … do you aim to be kind in all that you do? … what kinds of nice things have you done for others? … with all of these things that you have said, thought and done, God has been present … how do we know that God is present in the kindness we extend to those around us? …

Let us pray: O Holy Spirit, please help me to use your gifts to be kind to others in all that I think, all that I do, and all that I say … help me to be conscious of you working through me, and help me to draw closer to God … I ask this through Christ our Lord. Amen.

(Pause for about 10 to 20 seconds before giving the next set of instructions)

Bring your consciousness back to your focus words ... *Holy* ... *Spirit* ... Now, as you breathe in, concentrate on the word *Holy* ... and as you breathe out, concentrate on *Spirit* ... (*allow participants to take a few breaths*). Begin to wiggle your toes, your fingers. When you are ready, open your eyes and slowly sit up. Please remain quiet until we are ready to reflect on our meditation.

Reflection / Discussion Questions:

1. Write a thank-you letter or card to someone who has done an act of kindness for you.
2. Do you think kindness is easier for some people than it is for others? Why?
3. Draw something that you think symbolizes kindness. Explain why you chose this symbol.

Goodness

Track 7

Begin with the warm-up for this section, then move into the meditation:

What characteristics come to mind when you think of someone who is good? … for Christians, goodness is about choosing to do the right thing, to live our lives in a way that would bring joy to God … how do we know if we've chosen to do something good? … making good choices can be very challenging, but if we persist, and try our best to use the Gifts of the Holy Spirit in our everyday lives, we could all make the world a better place to live in … let us take a moment to meditate on this fruit of the Holy Spirit …

What are some good things you have done that you are proud of? … why are you proud of these things? … imagine that God is sitting with you right now … what would God say to you about your good and poor choices? … how would God encourage you to keep doing the good things that you do? … when you are challenged between making a good choice and a poor choice, what advice would God give you that could help you act lovingly? in other words, what strategies would God give you to help you make a good decision? …

Let us pray: O Holy Spirit, please help me to use your gifts to be a good person in all that I think, say and do …help me to be conscious of you working through me, and help me to draw closer to God … I ask this through Christ our Lord. Amen.

(Pause for about 10 to 20 seconds before giving the next set of instructions)

Bring your consciousness back to your focus words … *Holy* … *Spirit* … Now, as you breathe in, concentrate on the word *Holy* … and as you breathe out, concentrate on *Spirit* … (*allow participants to take a few breaths*). Begin to wiggle your toes, your fingers. When you are ready, open your eyes and slowly sit up. Please remain quiet until we are ready to reflect on our meditation.

Reflection / Discussion Questions:

1. Write down some of the strategies that God gave you to help you be good and loving. Add some of your own ideas as well.
2. Can a person be all good or all bad? How do you know?
3. Draw something that you think symbolizes goodness. Explain why you chose this symbol.

Generosity

Track 7

Begin with the warm-up for this section, then move into the meditation:

What does it mean to be generous? … as a young Catholic, you are constantly asked to be generous … being generous doesn't always mean giving lots of money to different charities … at school or at church, you may be asked to be generous towards social justice initiatives, and to be generous with your time, gifts and talents … when we're generous, we do more than what people expect from us, without thinking about how it can benefit ourselves … we choose to give more of our time, gifts and talents, more of our money or belongings, because it's something that we feel compelled to do, and because it makes those around us happy … let us take a moment to meditate on this fruit of the Holy Spirit …

Was there ever a time when you couldn't help but give to someone who needed your help? … perhaps you willingly spent more time than usual helping a younger sibling with some homework that they were having trouble with … or you used your talents to bring a smile to someone's face in your community … or maybe you were on a team to help raise money or awareness for a Catholic charity … whatever it was, what made you want to do those things and more? … how can giving something away – our time, talent and treasure – make us happy? … how does this bring us closer to God? …

Let us pray: O Holy Spirit, please help me to use your gifts to be generous with my time, talent and treasure … help me to be conscious of you working through me, and help me to draw closer to God ... I ask this through Christ our Lord. Amen.

(Pause for about 10 to 20 seconds before giving the next set of instructions)

Bring your consciousness back to your focus words ... *Holy* ... *Spirit* ... Now, as you breathe in, concentrate on the word *Holy* ... and as you breathe out, concentrate on *Spirit* ... (*allow participants to take a few breaths*). Begin to wiggle your toes, your fingers. When you are ready, open your eyes and slowly sit up. Please remain quiet until we are ready to reflect on our meditation.

Reflection / Discussion Questions:

1. Think of a person, or a character in a book, movie or TV show, who is generous. Why did you pick this person or character as an example?
2. Create a pamphlet encouraging other people to be generous. Share it with your classmates.
3. Draw something that you think symbolizes generosity. Explain why you chose this symbol.

Gentleness

Track 7

Begin with the warm-up for this section, then move into the meditation:

What comes to mind when you think of someone who is gentle? ... when we're gentle, we aren't necessarily weak ... in fact, it is quite the opposite ... Gentle people, like Jesus, know and understand what is right and wrong ... they have a way of explaining things, or standing up for something in a way that is kind and loving, rather than harsh and rude ... they aren't proud or arrogant ... in fact, they are the opposite of those things ... let us take a moment to reflect on this fruit of the Holy Spirit ...

Think of someone you know who is gentle ... (if you're stuck, Jesus is a great person to think of!) ... how does this person treat others? ... how do you feel when you are around them? ... what do you like about a person who is gentle? ... can you think of a time when you have behaved gently towards someone? ... how do you think it made the other person feel? ... now think of a time when you treated a person unkindly ... how do you think that person felt? ... it isn't always easy to be a gentle person, but with the help of God and the Holy Spirit, we can work on developing this fruit ...

Let us pray: O Holy Spirit, please help me to use your gifts to be generous with my time, talent and treasure ... help me to be conscious of you working through me, and help me to draw closer to God ... I ask this through Christ our Lord. Amen.

(Pause for about 10 to 20 seconds before giving the next set of instructions)

Bring your consciousness back to your focus words … *Holy* … *Spirit* … Now, as you breathe in, concentrate on the word *Holy* … and as you breathe out, concentrate on *Spirit* … (*allow participants to take a few breaths*). Begin to wiggle your toes, your fingers. When you are ready, open your eyes and slowly sit up. Please remain quiet until we are ready to reflect on our meditation.

Reflection / Discussion Questions:

1. A large part of being a gentle person is in the way we say things. With a partner, say each of the following phrases in a gentle way and in a not gentle way.
   - **a.** No, you can't borrow my pencil.
   - **b.** Nice hair.
   - **c.** You're good at that.
2. It is possible for gentle people to succeed in the world. Do you agree or disagree? Support your answer.
3. Draw something that you think symbolizes gentleness. Explain why you chose this symbol.

Faithfulness

Track 7

Begin with the warm-up for this section, then move into the meditation:

Have you ever felt like every bit of you, your mind and your heart and your soul, believed in something so much, you were positive that what you knew was right? … when we use the gifts of the Holy Spirit, faithfulness towards God is one of the fruits we exhibit … in other words, when our faith is strong, we are firm in our beliefs of God, his goodness and his work … we are loyal to God and strive to do good things … the people in our lives can see this fruit develop in us, as we grow to be more dependable and trustworthy … faithfulness, in many ways, helps us to believe in God in both good times and hard times … let us take a moment to meditate on this fruit of the Holy Spirit …

Think of someone you know who is faithful … what actions do they do that show they are loyal, or have a firm belief in something or someone? … do you have faith in God? … how do you know? … what actions could you take to further develop your faith in God? … God has faith in you whether you are at a point in your life when you have or don't have faith in him … why would God believe deeply in our ability to do good things, and be loyal and loving? … what is it about people that God finds joy in us? …

Let us pray: O Holy Spirit, please help me to use your gifts to be faithful to you … help me to be conscious of you working through me, and help me to draw closer to God … I ask this through Christ our Lord. Amen.

(Pause for about 10 to 20 seconds before giving the next set of instructions)

Bring your consciousness back to your focus words … *Holy* … *Spirit* … Now, as you breathe in, concentrate on the word *Holy* … and as you breathe out, concentrate on *Spirit* … (*allow participants to take a few breaths*). Begin to wiggle your toes, your fingers. When you are ready, open your eyes and slowly sit up. Please remain quiet until we are ready to reflect on our meditation.

Reflection / Discussion Questions:

1. Do you think having faith in God is something private, or is it something you need to share with others? Explain your thinking.
2. It's easier to have faith when things are going your way. Do you agree or disagree with this statement? Justify your answer.
3. Draw something that you think symbolizes gentleness. Explain why you chose this symbol.

Modesty

Track 7

Begin with the warm-up for this section, then move into the meditation:

We rarely hear people talk about modesty in our communities, with our friends or even in our families … for Catholics, to be modest takes into account our actions, our words, and also how we dress … to be modest means to act, speak and dress appropriately – specifically, to behave in a way that isn't too sexual or revealing … why? … because we believe that while our sexuality is part of being human, and a gift from God, our bodies and the bodies of other people need to be treated with dignity, respect and love … it may sound old-fashioned, but there is a lot of wisdom in showing a limited amount of our bodies, speaking appropriately, and limiting our public displays of affection … practising modesty can be tough, especially when everything around us seems to send the message that there's no need to be modest in today's world … just look at our TV shows, movies, music videos, magazines and advertisements, which blatantly showcase people's bodies … how often do we see modesty in these media? … let us take a moment to meditate on this fruit of the Holy Spirit …

Why would the Holy Spirit urge us to act reserved? … if you ever made inappropriate comments about others, what problems could arise for you? … what problems could arise for the people you spoke about in such a way? … have you ever wondered why there is a dress code at your school? … try to think of reasons why your school wants you to dress modestly, rather than wearing whatever you want … why does God want us to choose to be modest? … how do you think modesty can bring you closer to God? …

Let us pray: O Holy Spirit, please help me to use your gifts to be modest in my thoughts, words and clothing … help me to be conscious of you working through me, and help me to draw closer to God … I ask this through Christ our Lord. Amen.

(Pause for about 10 to 20 seconds before giving the next set of instructions)

Bring your consciousness back to your focus words … *Holy* … *Spirit* … Now, as you breathe in, concentrate on the word *Holy* … and as you breathe out, concentrate on *Spirit* … (*allow participants to take a few breaths*). Begin to wiggle your toes, your fingers. When you are ready, open your eyes and slowly sit up. Please remain quiet until we are ready to reflect on our meditation.

Reflection / Discussion Questions:

1. Think of an ad in a current magazine that is not very modest. Design a new ad that makes the same product appealing, but respects the model's body.
2. Modesty is a thing of the past. Do you agree or disagree? Why?
3. Draw something that you think symbolizes modesty. Explain why you chose this symbol.

Self-control

Track 7

Begin with the warm-up for this section, then move into the meditation:

As we get older, the adults around us expect that we develop self-control, because reckless, uncontrolled behaviour can get us into a lot of trouble and can even cause us or others to get hurt … God feels the same way, but he also wants us to use our self-control not just to avoid harm, but in a way that can help us do good things for our families, friends, communities and ourselves … we know that there are things in the world that tempt us to make poor choices … if you think about it, even Jesus was tempted to do things: to make stones into bread, jump off a mountain to have angels rescue him, and be given a ton of money, just to prove that he was the Son of God … but instead, Jesus chose to worship and love God … let us take a moment to reflect on this fruit of the Holy Spirit …

Think of a time when you have been tempted to do something that you knew was not a great choice … did you do it? or did you stop yourself? … why? … what were some of the consequences? … other than getting in trouble, why should young Catholics exercise self-control? … how does this benefit you? … how do the Gifts of the Holy Spirit help us to exercise self-control? …

Let us pray: O Holy Spirit, please help me to use your gifts to help me develop my self-control … help me to be conscious of you working through me, and help me to draw closer to God … I ask this through Christ our Lord. Amen.

(Pause for about 10 to 20 seconds before giving the next set of instructions)

Bring your consciousness back to your focus words … *Holy* … *Spirit* … Now, as you breathe in, concentrate on the word *Holy* … and as you breathe out, concentrate on *Spirit* … (*allow participants to take a few breaths*). Begin to wiggle your toes, your fingers. When you are ready, open your eyes and slowly sit up. Please remain quiet until we are ready to reflect on our meditation.

Reflection / Discussion Questions:

1. Write a commercial for self-control. Videotape it and share it with your class.
2. In your opinion, how can self-control lead you to be closer to God?
3. Draw something that you think symbolizes gentleness. Explain why you chose this symbol.

Chastity

Track 7

Begin with the warm-up for this section, then move into the meditation:

What do you think of when you hear the word "chastity"? … Chastity asks us to have control over our sexual impulses … God created us as sexual beings, and we are called to treat our bodies and the bodies of our neighbours with dignity and respect, always remembering that we are created as reflections of God … when we are asked to be chaste, it's about more than not having sexual intercourse … we are invited to have reverence for waiting, for discovering the beauty of the person we love beyond their physicality, but towards the essence of who they are … it isn't always easy, especially when we are surrounded by so many things that tell us that chastity is a thing of the past … let us take a moment to reflect on this fruit of the Holy Spirit …

Why do you think God wants us to wait to have sex? … what are some things we can learn about the person we are dating when we say no to sex? … how does this fruit bring us closer to God? …

Let us pray: O Holy Spirit, Please help me to use your gifts to help me to be chaste … help me to be conscious of you working through me, and help me to draw closer to God … I ask this through Christ our Lord. Amen.

(Pause for about 10 to 20 seconds before giving the next set of instructions)

Bring your consciousness back to your focus words … *Holy* … *Spirit* … Now, as you breathe in, concentrate on the word *Holy* … and as you breathe out, concentrate on *Spirit* … (*allow participants to take a few breaths*). Begin to wiggle your toes, your fingers. When you are ready, open your eyes and slowly sit up. Please remain quiet until we are ready to reflect on our meditation.

Reflection / Discussion Questions:

1. Create a brochure that encourages other young people to wait before having sex.
2. Create a pro and con list to being chaste. Reflect on what you discover when you make your list.
3. Draw something that you think symbolizes chastity.
   Explain why you chose this symbol.

Using the Fruits of the Holy Spirit

Track 7

Begin with the warm-up for this section, then move into the meditation:

When we use and develop the gifts that the Holy Spirit strengthens in us at Confirmation, we end up making choices to act in certain ways … these actions not only help us to see the work of the Holy Spirit in each of us, but also help to bring us closer to God … let us take a moment to reflect on each of the twelve fruits of the Holy Spirit …

How can you show *charity* to those around me? … in what ways are you a *joyful* person? … How can you help to bring *peace* to myself and others? … what are some strategies you can use to become more *patient* with people? … why do the Gifts of the Holy Spirit help you to treat people with love and *kindness*? … when you are faced with a decision, what are some things you could do to help you make *good choices*? … how are you *generous* with your time, talents and treasure? … what are some ways that you have treated people with *gentleness*? … how can you be more *faithful*? … what are some ways you can be *modest* in the way you dress, speak and act? … what ways can work to develop *self-control*? … in what ways can you work towards living a life that is *chaste*? …

Which fruits of the Holy Spirit best describe you? … which fruits of the Holy Spirit do you need to develop further? …

Let us pray: O Holy Spirit, please help me to use your gifts to help me to be chaste ... help me to be conscious of you working through me, and help me to draw closer to God ... I ask this through Christ our Lord. Amen.

(Pause for about 10 to 20 seconds before giving the next set of instructions)

Bring your consciousness back to your focus words ... *Holy* ... *Spirit* ... Now, as you breathe in, concentrate on the word *Holy* ... and as you breathe out, concentrate on *Spirit* ... (*allow participants to take a few breaths*). Begin to wiggle your toes, your fingers. When you are ready, open your eyes and slowly sit up. Please remain quiet until we are ready to reflect on our meditation.

Culminating Activities

1. Create your own guided meditation for one of the fruits of the Holy Spirit. Share it with your classmates.
2. In a group of four, create a poem about the fruits of the Holy Spirit. Perform it for the rest of the group.
3. Choose a symbol for each fruit of the Holy Spirit. Illustrate the symbols and make them into a book or slideshow, explaining why you chose each one. Or share your symbols with your classmates and see if they can guess what each symbol represents. Be prepared to explain why you chose these symbols.
4. Cut some pieces of paper into twelve strips. On each strip, write one of the fruits of the Holy Spirit. Place the strips in a bag and have members of the large group silently draw a strip of paper each. They then take turns miming actions that give clues for which fruit of the Spirit they drew. Have others guess which fruit of the Holy Spirit they are. Guessers need to be able to explain how they know they are right.

Lent and Easter

Note: *Invite participants to keep a journal for the whole Lenten season, documenting how they do with their Lenten devotion. Have them write about what they find easy and challenging about their devotion, ways that it's bringing them closer to God, and any other thoughts they have during Lent. This will be one of the culminating activities for this section.*

WARM-UP

Track 1 or Track 2

Find a comfortable position and settle in … (*allow participants some time to get comfortable*) … take a nice, deep breath and let the air flow slowly out of your lungs … do this again, paying special attention to the air as you inhale … and as you exhale … inhale … exhale … inhale … exhale … now, as you take a deep breath, I want you to hold it and scrunch up your toes as tightly as you can … breathe out and relax … this time, take a deep breath and flex your calves … hold it … and relax … deep breath and tighten your thighs … hold it … and relax … deep breath and tighten your stomach … hold it … and relax … take a deep breath and make the tightest fists possible … hold it … and relax … deep breath and stretch your arms until they're tight … hold it … and relax … now take a deep breath and bring your shoulders right up to your ears … hold it … and relax … take a deep breath and scrunch up your face … hold it … and relax … and take a deep breath and tense up your whole body … from the tips of your toes, through your legs, your stomach, your arms and your face … hold it … and relax … now, as you relax, concentrate on your breathing … inhale … exhale … inhale … exhale …

Ash Wednesday: As you inhale, think "Jesus" … and as you exhale, think "Jesus" … (*allow participants enough time to think of Jesus for a few breaths*) …

Palm Sunday: As you inhale, think "Jesus" … and as you exhale, think "Jesus" … (*allow participants enough time to think of Jesus for a few breaths*) …

Holy Thursday: As you inhale, think "Jesus" … and as you exhale, think "Jesus" … *(allow participants enough time to think of Jesus for a few breaths)* …

Good Friday: As you inhale, think "Jesus" … and as you exhale, think "Jesus" … *(allow participants enough time to think of Jesus for a few breaths)* …

Easter: As you inhale, think "peace" … and as you exhale, think "peace" … *(allow participants enough time to think of peace for a few breaths)* …

Pentecost / Confirmation: As you inhale, think "Holy" … and as you exhale, think "Spirit" … *(allow participants enough time to think of the Holy Spirit for a few breaths)* …

Ash Wednesday

Track 5

Begin with the warm-up for this section, then move into the meditation:

Ash Wednesday marks the beginning of the season of Lent … the leftover palms from last year's Palm Sunday celebration have been burned and turned into ashes for today's celebration … the person distributing the ashes on our foreheads dips his or her thumb into ashes and then marks a cross on our foreheads, saying something like this: "Turn away from sin and be faithful to the Gospel" … let us take a moment to meditate on the visible sign of our faith that we wear on our foreheads at the beginning of Lent …

When you receive your ashes, how does it make you feel … why? … why do you think it is important to have a visible sign, such as ashes, as a reminder of our faith in Jesus and all he has done for us? … have you spent time thinking about what you want to do for Lent this year? … take a moment to reflect on something you'd like to give up (whether a food you love or negative behaviours that harm your relationship with God, others or yourself), or a special act of service that you'd like to do for others, or something that may make you feel closer to God for the next forty days … how does this Lenten devotion help you to be a better Christian? … if it doesn't, consider revising what you hoped to do this year … does your Lenten devotion help you think of God? … why or why not? … forty days can feel like a long time … what is your plan to carry through your Lenten promise till Easter? … let us take some time to pray to ask God to help us carry through our Lenten devotions …

Dear God, today is Ash Wednesday ... I hope that the ashes help to remind me of the love you have for me, my family, my friends and the world ... Please help me to stay committed to the Lenten devotion I have chosen to do this year ... Thank you, God. Amen.

(Pause for about 10 to 20 seconds before giving the next set of instructions)

Bring your consciousness back to your focus word ... *Jesus* ... Now, as you breathe in, concentrate on the name *Jesus* ... and as you breathe out, concentrate on *Jesus* ... (*allow participants to take a few breaths*). Begin to wiggle your toes, your fingers. When you are ready, open your eyes and slowly sit up. Please remain quiet until we are ready to reflect on our meditation.

Reflection / Discussion Questions:

1. Do you like receiving ashes on Ash Wednesday? Justify your answer.
2. What have you decided to do for Lent this year? What is your plan of action to carry through your Lenten devotion for the next forty days?
3. How would you explain Ash Wednesday to a person who isn't Catholic?

Palm Sunday

Track 5

Begin with the warm-up for this section, then move into the meditation:

Holy Week is the most important week for our faith, and Palm Sunday starts it off … it's the day that Jesus arrived in Jerusalem on a donkey … the people of the city cheered, laying palm branches on the road as he entered … today, we commemorate this event with the blessing of the palms, which are then handed out to everyone at church on Palm Sunday … let us take a moment to reflect on this special day …

Imagine that you are in Jerusalem during Jesus' time … you and your friends are gathering at the gate of the city with palm branches to welcome Jesus, who is arriving on a donkey … it's a big deal for you, because this is the sign God said he would send when the person who was going to save the world was here … who wouldn't feel happy if someone was going to come and make the world a better place? … after finding a spot on the road, you set down your branch and glance up at the crowd … the hot sun blazes down on the people who are cheering and chattering away with each other in excitement, not paying attention to the heat of the day … here is a great feeling of love in the air … everyone is happy … and then you see him … Jesus, the teacher, is approaching! … you stand on your tiptoes to see if you can get a better view of him … as he passes, he sees you and looks you straight in the eye … and for a brief moment, you see in his eyes that the excitement and happiness here in Jerusalem is not going to last … which doesn't really make much sense to you, because everyone around you is so happy! ... but Jesus smiles at you and lets you know with that small gesture that everything will be all right ... you and your friends watch until Jesus enters the Temple ... after he is out of your sight, you gather up your belongings and head home ...

(Pause for about 10 to 20 seconds before giving the next set of instructions)

Bring your consciousness back to your focus word ... *Jesus* ... Now, as you breathe in, concentrate on the name *Jesus* ... and as you breathe out, concentrate on *Jesus* ... (*allow participants to take a few breaths*). Begin to wiggle your toes, your fingers. When you are ready, open your eyes and slowly sit up. Please remain quiet until we are ready to reflect on our meditation.

Reflection / Discussion Questions:

1. How did you feel when you saw Jesus?
2. If you could have spoken to him when he arrived in Jerusalem, what would you have said to him?
3. Write a poem that captures the feeling in the crowd as Jesus arrived.

Holy Thursday

Track 5 or Track 6

Begin with the warm-up for this section, then move into the meditation:

Today is Holy Thursday ... it's a special day because on this day, we remember the Last Supper, the first time the Holy Eucharist was celebrated ... tonight, in churches all over the world, there will be re-enactments of Jesus washing his disciples' feet, and we will hear the story of how Jesus shared a meal with his closest friends, was betrayed by one of them, and eventually was arrested and taken into custody ... let us take a moment to think about Jesus, his disciples, and the last meal they shared together ...

Imagine that you are one of Jesus' disciples ... it is the night of the Passover, and you, Jesus, and the other disciples have gathered to share the Passover meal ... as you sit around the table, you notice that Jesus is quiet and lost in his thoughts ... he gets up from the table, removes his outer robe, pours water into a large basin and begins to wash your feet ... you look at your friends, confused ... you wait, knowing that Jesus will explain what he is doing when he is finished ... a silence falls over you and your friends ... when it is Simon Peter's turn, you hear Peter protest, "*You will never wash my feet.*" ... Jesus responds, "*Unless I wash you, you have no share with me ...*" ... so Peter lets Jesus wash his feet ... When Jesus is done with all the disciples, he says, "*Do you know what I have done to you? I have set you an example, that you also should do as I have done to you ...*" ... he sits down, and you all begin your meal ... at one point, Jesus says, "*Truly I tell you, one of you will betray me ...*" ... you look at Jesus and say, "*Not me, Lord … it can't be me!*" … it breaks your heart to think that Jesus would think one of you would do something to hurt him … everyone in the room also begins to deny that they will be the one who will betray Jesus … after things settle down, Jesus picks up a loaf of bread and says, "*Take this and eat; this is my body …*" … he passes it around and you do as Jesus says … then Jesus picks up the cup of wine and says, "*Take this, and drink from it; this is my blood …*" … he passes the cup around and you each take a sip … when supper is finished and tidied up, you, the disciples and Jesus gather your things and prepare to go to the garden, where Jesus wants to pray … you feel a bit uneasy, but push the feeling aside as you get up to go and follow Jesus …

(Pause for about 10 to 20 seconds before giving the next set of instructions)

Bring your consciousness back to your focus word … *Jesus* … Now, as you breathe in, concentrate on the name *Jesus* … and as you breathe out, concentrate on *Jesus* … (*allow participants to take a few breaths*). Begin to wiggle your toes, your fingers. When you are ready, open your eyes and slowly sit up. Please remain quiet until we are ready to reflect on our meditation.

Reflection / Discussion Questions:

1. How did you feel when Jesus washed your feet? Explain your thinking.
2. When Jesus said that one of your friends would betray him, how did you feel? Why?
3. We remember the Last Supper every time we go to Mass and the priest prays the Eucharistic Prayer. Why do you think the Last Supper is important for Catholics?

Good Friday

Track 6

Begin with the warm-up for this section, then move into the meditation:

Only a few hours have passed since Jesus walked the streets of Jerusalem, carrying his cross … you let your mind drift to the different scenes of the day … Jesus struggling to carry the heavy cross … people jeering at him … watching Jesus and his mother, suspended in time as they looked lovingly at each other as he walked by … all along, with these intimate and personal moments with Jesus, there was so much noise and movement … Jesus falling … the soldiers pushing … the crowd cheering … they wanted to see someone suffer … it feels surreal that these moments following Jesus' death are so eerily quiet … other than the storm brewing in the distance, there is little movement in Jerusalem … people rushed home after the scene, quick to prepare for the Sabbath … now, the streets are empty, silent … and here you are, with your thoughts, walking the dusty roads of Jerusalem, wondering, what now? … where do I go from here? … you look up and realize that you are alone … your friends have all scattered … many are scared … in your heart you feel despair … how can life be so unfair? … how can God take away someone you love? … you look down at your sandals and wiggle your toes … you remember that just a short while ago, Jesus was washing his disciples' feet at their last supper together … you glance up, realizing there are good memories of Jesus all around you … you catch yourself smiling and wonder … is it okay to smile when I feel so sad? … what did Jesus do to deserve this? … if God loves us so much, why do any of us have to suffer? … you know that there is no easy answer to these questions, but you begin to search your heart and ask yourself what the Lord would say to you about your feelings ... before all of this drama began, Jesus spoke of conquering death ... how can he do that? ... frustrated, you scream in your head, "I just don't understand!" ... you think of an earlier conversation when you and your friends asked him about entering heaven ... he said, "*It is easier for a camel to go through the eye of a needle than for someone who is rich to enter the kingdom of God ...*" and your friends asked, "*Then who can be saved?*" Jesus replied, "*For mortals it is impossible, but for God, all things are possible.*" ... you take a moment to reflect on what Jesus said: *for God, all things are possible* ... with God we can feel grief, sadness and despair ... but maybe, after some time has passed, with God things will feel different ... maybe, as impossible as it seems, the sadness you feel will lift ... you look up and realize you have arrived home ... you take off your sandals, wipe your feet and greet your family.

(Pause for about 10 to 20 seconds before giving the next set of instructions)

Bring your consciousness back to your focus word ... *Jesus* ... Now, as you breathe in, concentrate on the name *Jesus* ... and as you breathe out, concentrate on *Jesus* ... (*allow participants to take a few breaths*). Begin to wiggle your toes, your fingers. When you are ready, open your eyes and slowly sit up. Please remain quiet until we are ready to reflect on our meditation.

Reflection / Discussion Questions:

1. What emotions did you feel as you reflected on Jesus' death on Good Friday? Do you think it's okay to feel that way? Why or why not?
2. As Christians, we believe that death is not the end – those who die begin a new life with God. Why is it hard to remember this when someone we love dies? What support can you give yourself or others at times like this?
3. How would our lives be different if we truly believed that for God, all things are possible?

Easter

Track 7 or Track 9

Easter is the most important feast in the Christian faith because on that day, Jesus rises from the dead and overcomes death forever … by doing this, Jesus gives us life! … let us take a moment to reflect on Easter …

Imagine that it is the third day after Jesus' death … rumour has it that Mary Magdalene saw the Lord early in the morning, but you find that hard to believe … as you and a friend walk to the house of another disciple, you run into a man who asks what you are talking about … was he the only person in the whole city who didn't know all that had happened to Jesus the Nazarene? … you describe all of the events that happened this past week … from Palm Sunday to the last supper you shared with Jesus … from the awful time in the garden, where Jesus was arrested, to his carrying his cross through the streets on his way to be crucified … you then tell this stranger that Jesus said he would overcome death on the third day after he died … and despite the rumour that Mary Magdalene saw him, nothing extraordinary has been proven … as the three of you approach your destination, you ask the stranger if he'd like to come in for a meal … he accepts, and enters the home with you and your friend … sitting at the table, the man looks at you, your friend and the other disciples who had gathered for the meal … he picks up a loaf of bread and blesses it … the way he blessed the bread reminds you of your last meal with Jesus … you close your eyes and think, "This can't be a coincidence …" … you open your eyes and look carefully at the stranger in front of you … and you realize that he is no stranger … you gasp and you realize you've been with the Lord the whole time … your eyes meet for a brief moment and then Jesus disappears …

(Pause for about 10 to 20 seconds before giving the next set of instructions)

Bring your consciousness back to your focus word … Jesus … Now, as you breathe in, concentrate on the name *Jesus* … and as you breathe out, concentrate on *Jesus* … *(allow participants to take a few breaths)*. Begin to wiggle your toes, your fingers. When you are ready, open your eyes and slowly sit up. Please remain quiet until we are ready to reflect on our meditation.

Reflection / Discussion Questions:

1. Why was it hard to believe that something extraordinary might have happened three days after Jesus' death?
2. Describe how you felt when you realized the stranger was Jesus.
3. Why is it important to remember that our Christian story doesn't end with Good Friday? Why is Jesus' resurrection so important and central to our faith?

Pentecost / Confirmation

Track 7 or Track 9

Begin with the warm-up for this section, then move into the meditation:

Before Jesus ascended into heaven, he spoke to his disciples ... he told them to stay in Jerusalem, because the Holy Spirit was coming to baptize them ... when we are confirmed, the Holy Spirit also comes upon us and helps us to become better Christians, if we choose to do so ... let us take a moment to meditate on Pentecost and the coming of the Holy Spirit ...

Imagine that you are sitting with the disciples ... it is shortly after Jesus ascended into heaven ... and as he instructed, you all stay in Jerusalem to wait for the Holy Spirit to come ... suddenly, before any of you can react, you hear an extremely strong gust of wind blow through the house ... tongues of fire seem to rest above each person's head ... to your surprise, as one touches you, you begin to speak in another language ... "How can this be happening?" you ask yourself ... incredulously, you call out to the other disciples and they respond to you, each in a different language, and you understand them ... you try to read their faces, and a smile begins to emerge on your face ... "It has happened," you call out excitedly, "just as the Lord said it would!" ... at this point, people begin to arrive to check out what is going on in the house, because they had heard a very loud noise ... many of them were visiting Jerusalem ... many of them did not speak the same language as you and the other disciples because they were from out of town ... to your delight, each of you was able to communicate with the others! ... and with that, you, along with the other disciples, began to give witness to those around you about the Good News, in the hope that they, too, might believe in Jesus Christ.

Now take a moment to think of your Confirmation … what do/did you expect to happen when you receive/received the Holy Spirit? … on your special day, are/were you ready to say, "Yes! I believe in God the Father, in Jesus Christ, and in the Holy Spirit!" with your whole heart and mind? … how can you work to develop the gifts that the Holy Spirit bestows on you? … who can help you when you're struggling with your faith? … how do you intend to spread the Good News? … Now take some time to say a private prayer asking God to help you as you prepare to receive the sacrament of Confirmation/asking God to continue to guide you as you develop from being a young Catholic into a Catholic adult …

(Pause for about 10 to 20 seconds before giving the next set of instructions)

Bring your consciousness back to your focus words … *Holy* … *Spirit* … Now, as you breathe in, concentrate on the word *Holy* … and as you breathe out, concentrate on *Spirit* … (*allow participants to take a few breaths*). Begin to wiggle your toes, your fingers. When you are ready, open your eyes and slowly sit up. Please remain quiet until we are ready to reflect on our meditation.

Reflection / Discussion Questions:

1. How did you feel when the Holy Spirit came during your meditation? What would you do if the same thing happened to you today?
2. How do you share the Good News of God's love at home? at school? in your community?
3. Which is your favourite gift of the Holy Spirit in Confirmation? Why?

Culminating Activities

1. Invite participants to keep a journal for the whole Lenten season, documenting how they do with their Lenten devotion. Have them write about what they find easy and challenging about their devotion, ways that it's bringing them closer to God, and any other thoughts they have during Lent.
2. As a group, celebrate a Mass or a Liturgy of the Word during the Easter season. Find ways for everyone to be involved.

Faith in Action

WARM-UP

Track 1 or Track 2

Find a comfortable position and settle in … (*allow participants some time to get comfortable*) … take a nice, deep breath and let the air flow slowly out of your lungs … do this again, paying special attention to the air as you inhale … and as you exhale … inhale … exhale … inhale … exhale … now, as you take a deep breath, I want you to hold it and scrunch up your toes as tightly as you can … breathe out and relax … this time, take a deep breath and flex your calves … hold it … and relax … deep breath and tighten your thighs … hold it … and relax … deep breath and tighten your stomach … hold it … and relax … take a deep breath and make the tightest fists possible … hold it … and relax … deep breath and stretch your arms until they're tight … hold it … and relax … now take a deep breath and bring your shoulders right up to your ears … hold it … and relax … take a deep breath and scrunch up your face … hold it … and relax … and take a deep breath and tense up your whole body … from the tips of your toes, through your legs, your stomach, your arms and your face … hold it … and relax … now, as you relax, concentrate on your breathing … inhale … exhale … inhale … exhale …

The Commissioning of the Disciples: As you inhale, think "Jesus" … and as you exhale, think "Jesus" … *(allow participants enough time to think of Jesus for a few breaths)* …

Social Justice: As you inhale, think "love" … and as you exhale, think "love" … *(allow participants enough time to think of love for a few breaths)* …

Thanksgiving: As you inhale, think "thank" … and as you exhale, think "you" … *(allow participants enough time to think of being thankful for a few breaths)* …

Reconciliation: As you inhale, think "forgiveness" … and as you exhale, think "forgiveness" … *(allow participants enough time to think of forgiveness for a few breaths)* …

The Commissioning of the Disciples

Track 9

It is one of the days following Jesus' death and resurrection … you are one of his disciples, and you go with the others to Galilee to climb the mountain Jesus asked you to climb … as you walk up the mountain, you notice the chatter among you and your friends begin to dwindle … you start thinking about what has happened over the past few days … you think about Jesus' arrival in Jerusalem and how the people all celebrated … you remember the last supper you had with Jesus … you painfully remember later that night when he was arrested, interrogated and beaten … you think about the horrible day when he was crucified … and how three days later, Jesus rose from the dead! … you reflect on how your heart rejoiced when you saw and heard Jesus for the first time …

Your thoughts are interrupted when just ahead is the Lord … you cannot help but smile … you move quickly to catch up … Jesus smiles and says, "*All authority in heaven and on earth has been given to me … therefore, go and make disciples of all nations … baptizing them in the name of the Father, and of the Son, and of the Holy Spirit … teach them to obey everything that I have commanded you … and remember … I am with you always, to the end of the age …*"

Afterwards, Jesus sits down and asks, "Do you understand what I have just said? … you tell him that you're a bit confused, and he explains it to you …

you tell him your worries … but Lord, I am just a kid … I am afraid … what if people make fun of me? … Lord, this is a difficult challenge … why me? … Jesus looks you right in the eye and says to you, "Do not be afraid … for I know the plans I have for you … plans for your welfare and not for harm … to give you a future with hope … then, when you call upon me and come and pray to me, I will hear you … when you search for me, you will find me … if you seek me with all your heart, I will let you find me … for I will be with you always" … he gives you a hug and continues to visit with each of your friends …

You continue to sit on the ground, deep in thought … eventually you get up and begin to make your way back down the mountain … as you get to the bottom of the mountain, you realize the task ahead of you and you feel encouraged … you take comfort knowing that Jesus will always be with you … while you may not always understand how you will share with others the Word of God, he has great plans for you … and so you take your final step off the mountain and continue on your journey.

(Pause for about 10 to 20 seconds before giving the next set of instructions)

Bring your consciousness back to your focus word … *Jesus* … Now, as you breathe in, concentrate on the name *Jesus* … and as you breathe out, concentrate on *Jesus* … (*allow participants to take a few breaths*). Begin to wiggle your toes, your fingers. When you are ready, open your eyes and slowly sit up. Please remain quiet until we are ready to reflect on our meditation.

Reflection / Discussion Questions:

1. How do you feel about Jesus sending you out to teach others about all the things he teaches us? Explain your thinking.
2. Are there things that make you nervous about teaching people about God? How can you overcome these?
3. Where can you find support in your journey as a disciple?

Social Justice

Track 9

Begin with the warm-up for this section, then move into the meditation:

When you hear the words "social justice," what kinds of things come to mind? … Jesus' Sermon on the Mount gives us a new way of thinking, the Beatitudes … he tells us how we can help to care for those who are in need … let us take a moment to meditate on each of the Beatitudes …

Imagine that you are up on the mountain with your friends listening to Jesus speak … ***Blessed are the poor in spirit, for theirs is the kingdom of heaven*** … how can you share your gifts and talents with those around you? … how can you use your gifts and talents to show people that we can live God's kingdom here on earth right now? … ***Blessed are those who mourn, for they will be comforted*** … do I turn to God in times when I am sad and distressed? Why or why not? … how will I turn to God when the people around me are struggling? … ***Blessed are the meek, for they will inherit the earth*** … in what ways can I be gentle and kind to the people around me? … how can I treat others with love and respect, and recognize that all people are children of God? … ***Blessed are those who hunger and thirst for righteousness, for they will be filled*** … who do I feel drawn to help? … what can I do to try to make the world a better place and a fair place to live? … ***Blessed are the merciful, for they will receive mercy*** … do I try to forgive people who have done hurtful things? … can I show compassion to others who have done something wrong? … ***Blessed are the pure in heart, for they will see God*** … you take a moment to think of the good things you have done in your life and ask yourself, how can I continue to do God's work? ... ***Blessed are the peacemakers, for they will be called children of God*** ... *do I make an effort to find ways to resolve conflict peacefully? ... do I help others to grow in dignity and respect for themselves and the people around them?* ... ***Blessed are those who are persecuted for righteousness' sake, for theirs is the kingdom of heaven*** ... do I strive to do what's right, even though people might make fun of me? ... am I prepared to take that risk? ... ***Blessed are you when people revile you and persecute you and utter all kinds of evil against you falsely on my account. Rejoice and be glad, for your reward is great in heaven*** ... will I let people know that I'm a follower of Jesus? ... can I do this and rejoice, even if people say mean things about me? ... it will be a challenge to follow through with all of these things ... but there's never any harm in trying your best ... and you know Jesus will be with you to guide you.

(Pause for about 10 to 20 seconds before giving the next set of instructions)

Bring your consciousness back to your focus word ... *love* ... Now, as you breathe in, concentrate on the word *love* ... and as you breathe out, concentrate on *love* ... (*allow participants to take a few breaths*). Begin to wiggle your toes, your fingers. When you are ready, open your eyes and slowly sit up. Please remain quiet until we are ready to reflect on our meditation.

Reflection / Discussion Questions:

Before asking these questions, write the Beatitudes on a blackboard or poster for the group to see.

1. Which are your favourite Beatitudes? Choose at least three and explain your choices.
2. Write your own version of the Beatitudes for young Catholics today.
3. Do you think any of the Beatitudes are difficult to do? Explain your answer.

Thanksgiving

Track 9

Begin with the warm-up for this section, then move into the meditation:

How often do we take time to pause and say thank you for the things we have, the things we can do, and, most importantly the people we love? ... Thanksgiving is a great time to pause in our busy lives to think and thank God, our family and our friends for all they do to enrich our lives ... let us take a moment to reflect on giving thanks as we prepare for Thanksgiving weekend ...

What are some things that you are most grateful for this year? ... now take each of these thoughts and reflect on why you are grateful for them ... how would your life be different without these things? ... take some time and imagine telling a person you care about how thankful you are for them ... be specific as you list and describe why you are grateful to have this person in your life ... What do they do that is so special? ... what are some things about yourself that you are thankful for? ... perhaps you're thankful for skills that you have, personality traits that you possess, or even the way you look ... the things we have, the people in our lives and who we are as individuals are gifts from God ... take a moment to say thank you to God for all that you have thought about during this time ... it can be in a prayer, or a conversation, or even a mental email or text message ... what's important is to let God know why you are so thankful for these wonderful things ...

(Pause for about 10 to 20 seconds before giving the next set of instructions)

Bring your consciousness back to your focus words … *thank you* … Now, as you breathe in, concentrate on the word *thank* … and as you breathe out, concentrate on the word *you* … (*allow participants to take a few breaths*). Begin to wiggle your toes, your fingers. When you are ready, open your eyes and slowly sit up. Please remain quiet until we are ready to reflect on our meditation.

Reflection / Discussion Questions:

1. What are some things you're thankful for today?
2. Who was the person that you wanted to thank? Why did you choose him or her?
3. What were some of the things you thanked God for? Why?

Reconciliation

Track 9

Begin with the warm-up for this section, then move into the meditation:

Reconciliation means mending a relationship that has been broken in some way ... reconciling with someone can be very difficult, because when we apologize for doing something wrong or hurting someone's feelings, we have to admit to our own faults ... we have to say out loud that what we did was not a Christian thing to do ... or we have to forgive someone who has hurt us, and learn to trust them again ... the sacrament of Reconciliation helps us to keep an open and honest relationship with God ... God loves us no matter what, but letting him know that we know we could have handled things better in our lives helps us draw closer to God, and also helps us grow as Catholics as we strive be better people ... let us take a moment to reflect on reconciliation, love and forgiveness ...

Think of a time when you got into a fight with someone ... what started it? ... what emotions did you feel? ... what happened after your argument? ... did either of you apologize? ... how do you know when things are better between you and your friends or family? ... when we go to the sacrament of Reconciliation, we are asked to reflect on all aspects of our lives ... we know we have done good things, but we also know that there are things we need to try to do better ... let us now meditate on the following questions ...

Do I love God with my whole heart, mind and soul, or have I sometimes shown a love for popularity, owning things, or money? ... have I ever used God's name inappropriately? ... do I go to Mass on Sunday? … have I been loving and kind to my parents or guardians? … have I taken time to say thank you for what they do for me? … have I taken care of my body and treated it with love and respect? … have I been kind to others? … have I been jealous of what others have? … are there any things in my heart and mind that I'd like to say I'm sorry for, but haven't yet? …

Dear God, I know that you love me unconditionally … please help me with the things that I struggle with, but also help me to recognize the good things I do … please give me the courage to recognize the times that I need to celebrate the sacrament of Reconciliation … Thank you, God.

(Pause for about 10 to 20 seconds before giving the next set of instructions)

Bring your consciousness back to your focus word … *forgiveness* … Now, as you breathe in, concentrate on the word *forgiveness* … and as you breathe out, concentrate on *forgiveness* … (*allow participants to take a few breaths*). Begin to wiggle your toes, your fingers. When you are ready, open your eyes and slowly sit up. Please remain quiet until we are ready to reflect on our meditation.

Reflection / Discussion Questions:

1. Which do you find more challenging: to forgive others or to be forgiven?
2. Is there someone you need to reconcile with? How could you start the process?
3. Did you learn anything about yourself during this meditation? If so, what did you learn?

Culminating Activities

1. As a group, create a "Faith in Action Fair" that showcases different Catholic organizations that help those in need within your community and in the larger world. Be creative! You could make posters, perform skits or design websites. Share your findings with your school, youth group or parish, or invite people from your area to attend.

2. Create a commercial that encourages people to take action within their communities to be thankful, forgiving or active in helping others. Share your message with others.

Notes

Notes

Notes

Notes

Notes

Bestselling Resources for School Prayer & Worship from Novalis

School Liturgies Made Easy

By Lisa Freemantle & Carmela Caporiccio

Drawing from extensive experience preparing for school liturgies as teachers, the authors provide all the tools necessary for preparing for a Mass or a Prayer Service. This excellent resources describes the various parts of the Mass and gives practical, easy-to-use ideas for setting up for liturgy, selecting music and involving students, all for the purpose of creating meaningful liturgies.

96pp PB 978-2-89646-408-1 $16.95

Prayers for the School Year

By Rosanna Golino

An outstanding collection of prayer services set according to the liturgical seasons and feast days. With the daily cycle of Lectionary readings as the central focus, these prayer services may be used in many settings including classroom prayer, retreats or school assemblies. Engage all your students in deep and meaningful prayer appropriate to their life experience.

320pp PB 978-2-89507-484-7 $39.95

NOVALIS

www.novalis.ca

Bestselling Resources for School Prayer & Worship from Novalis

Words for the Journey

By Lisa Freemantle & Les Miller

Designed to foster spiritual experiences within Catholic school communities, these original, ready-to-use ten-minute prayer services can be used as introductions to staff meetings, at the beginning or closing events at PA days, during informal staff gatherings or as stand-alone prayer services.

144pp PB 978-2-89646-142-4 $24.95

Words for the Journey for Kids

By Lisa Freemantle & Les Miller

Words for the Journey for Kids is perfect for the classroom. Each fun, easy-to-use service has simple ideas for set up and is divided into separate reader's sections. All the themes are firmly rooted in the Word of God, and each prayer service contains a reading adapted from the *Good News Bible.*

96pp PB 978-2-89646-239-1 $19.95

Words for the Journey for Teens

By Lisa Freemantle, Les Miller & Melinda Rapallo-Ferrara

Words for the Journey for Teens is a perfect book for the classroom. Each inviting, easy-to-use service has simple ideas for set-up and is divided into sections for individual readers. Organized by month from September to June, this book can be used in either a classroom or a whole-school setting. Some of the services are designed with parts for the students to act out, while others are more contemplative.

96pp PB 978-2-89646-303-9 $19.95

NOVALIS

www.novalis.ca